D0041709

TWAYNE'S WORLD AUTHORS SERIES

A Survey of the World's Literature

Sylvia E. Bowman, Indiana University

GENERAL EDITOR

FRANCE

Maxwell A. Smith, Guerry Professor of French, Emeritus
The University of Chattanooga
Visiting Professor in Modern Languages
The Florida State University

EDITOR

Albert Camus

TWAS 69

TWAYNE'S WORLD AUTHORS SERIES (TWAS)

*The purpose of TWAS is to survey the major writers
—novelists, dramatists, historians, poets, philosophers,
and critics—of the nations of the world. Among the
national literatures covered are those of Australia,
Canada, China, Eastern Europe, France, Germany,
Greece, Italy, Japan, Latin America, New Zealand,
Poland, Russia, Scandinavia, Spain, and the African
nations, as well as Hebrew, Yiddish, and Latin Classical literature. This survey is complemented by
Twayne's United States Authors Series and
English Authors Series.*

*The intent of each volume in these series is to present
a critical-analytical study of the works of the writer;
to include biographical and historical material that
may be necessary for understanding, appreciation,
and critical appraisal of the writer; and to present all
material in clear, concise English—but not to vitiate
the scholarly content of the work by doing so.*

Albert Camus

By PHILLIP H. RHEIN
Vanderbilt University

TWAYNE PUBLISHERS
A DIVISION OF G. K. HALL & CO., BOSTON

Library of Congress Catalog Card Number: 69-18497
ISBN 0-8057-2196-7

TO MY PARENTS

Contents

About the Author

Phillip H. Rhein, Chairman of the Comparative Literature program at Vanderbilt University, received his graduate training at Washington University in St. Louis and at the University of Michigan in Ann Arbor. Dr. Rhein directed the Vanderbilt in France program in Aix-en-Provence in 1964 and while in France, had the opportunity to meet Madame Camus and to discuss some of the material of this book with her. Professor Rhein's *The Urge to Live*, a comparative analysis of Kafka and Camus appeared in 1964 and has received general critical acclaim.

Preface

On January 4, 1960, Camus was killed in an automobile accident while returning to Paris from Lourmarin. During the intervening years his words have retained their vitality, and they speak to a new generation of young intellectuals with the same intensity that they had for their fathers.

I am sure that the reasons for the existence of Camus' popularity among young people today are manifold. However, among all the possible reasons, the most outstanding one is the simple truth that even in an age so swiftly-paced that ideas and ideologies are overthrown in a moment, in a decade that foresees man's conquest of the moon, many things have remained constant. Twenty years ago the actions of a Roosevelt, a Stalin, or a Churchill dominated the front pages of our newspapers; today the headlines are captured by new feats in space or old facets of the Cold War. The frug has replaced the jitterbug: Louis Armstrong is an unknown alongside the Beatles; James Bond is the new romantic hero; but when the younger generation switches from entertainment to serious conversation and discusses the meaning of life and the goal of mankind, the differences between their problems and those of their fathers are extremely meager.

During the closing months of World War II, their fathers spent their existentialist apprenticeship in reading Kafka, Sartre's *La Nausée*, and Camus' *L'Etranger*. In these writings they found their own complex life of solitude, slavery, and freedom rendered intelligible. Philosophy was brought down to earth for them and the anguish that they experienced was given a name and better understood. In their endless conversations they rebuilt the world—richer, more just, more sincere—where the right to pursue happiness would be a living reality rather than a vague constitutional right. Never had they felt so joyous or so confident in the future of mankind.

The children of these men, not quite so fresh, never so adolescent, grapple with the same intellectual problems. Many of them have keener insight into the suffering of others and a more serious concern for world justice. Reared on the truths of Hiroshima, the Berlin Wall, oppression, food shortages, and race riots, they cannot share their fathers' confidence in the future of mankind. The intervening years have brought scientific but not humanistic progress.

Today the young intellectual seeks to understand rather than rebuild the world. Although he may never sit in the smoky warmth of the Café de Flore and await undisturbed the late afternoon arrival of Camus after his work at Gallimard's, if time could be recaptured, the tone of the meetings and the conversations between Camus and him would be much the same. There would be no attempt on Camus' part to enlist a disciple—he never conceived of himself as a master —rather he would listen and hope that through expression he would somehow assist in the growth of the young man's freedom. Camus firmly believed that no one can begin his philosophic education at the end. Each man must experience for himself the philosopher's progress to wisdom; for without personal involvement and understanding, there can be no true philosophic development.

This one fact alone perhaps more than any other accounts for Camus' wide appeal throughout the world today. His thought and his art are evolving things that proceed from personal thoughts and experiences to a philosophic view of the world that corresponds exactly to the prevailing universal mood since 1942. According to Camus,

One lives with a few familiar ideas. Two or three. By the chance of worlds and men who are encountered, one polishes them and transforms them. It takes ten years to have an idea fully one's own—about which one can talk. Naturally, this is a little discouraging. But in this way man gains a certain familiarity with the beautiful face of the world. Up to that point he looked at it face to face. But then he has to step to the side to gaze at its profile. A young man looks at the world face to face. He hasn't had the time to polish the idea of death and nothingness, the horror of which, however, he has tasted.[1]

The "few familiar ideas" investigated and developed by Camus gradually evolve into an art and thought that is undeniably his own.[2]

PHILLIP H. RHEIN

Vanderbilt University

Acknowledgments

I thank the following American publishers for permission to quote from books by and about Camus.

From Camus' works: Random House, Inc. (New York) for *Resistance, Rebellion, and Death; The Myth of Sisyphus; The Stranger; Caligula and Three Other Plays; The Plague; The Rebel; The Fall;* and *The Exile and the Kingdom.*

From works about Camus: The University of North Carolina Press (Chapel Hill) for *The Urge to Live* by Phillip H. Rhein; *Partisan Review* for "Sartre versus Camus: A Political Quarrel" by Nicola Chiaromonte; The *Reporter Magazine* for "Tribute to Albert Camus" by Jean-Paul Sartre; and George Braziller, Inc. (New York) for *Albert Camus: The Invincible Summer* by Albert Maquet.

Chronology

1913   Born November 7 in Mondovi, Algeria, of Lucien and Catherine Sintès Camus.

1914   Father killed in Battle of the Marne, World War I.

1918–   Attends grade school at L'École communale de la rue Au-
1923   merat in Algiers.

1923–   Scholarship student at the Lycée of Algiers.
1930

1930   Student of philosophy at University of Algiers; first serious
attack of tuberculosis interrupts his preparation for career in
college teaching; for next several years supports himself with
a series of odd jobs.

1932   Continues to pursue his studies under Jean Grenier to whom
he later dedicated *La Mort dans l'âme, L'Envers et l'endroit,
L'Homme révolté;* publishes four articles in the review *Sud.*

1934   A brief first marriage ending in divorce a year later.

1934–   Membership in Communist party, with which he is soon dis-
1935   enchanted.

1935   Actor-director-playwright in Théâtre du Travail, which he
founds; production of *La Révolte dans les Asturies,* of which
he is part author.

1936   Receives the *diplôme d'études supérieures* in philosophy.

1936–   Engaged as an actor by Radio-Algiers.
1937

1937   Théâtre du Travail becomes the Théâtre de l'Equipe; publica-
tion of *L'Envers et l'endroit (Betwixt and Between);* visits
Florence, Genoa, and Pisa; becomes journalist for the *Alger
Républicain,* edited by Pascal Pia to whom he later dedicated
Le Mythe de Sisyphe.

1938   Writes *Caligula;* works on an essay on the absurd; reassembles
his notes for *L'Etranger.*

1939   Publication of *Noces (Nuptials);* trip to Oran.

1940   Second marriage, to Francine Faure, in Lyon; completes *L'Etranger* in May.

1941   Returns to Oran in January; completes *Le Mythe de Sisyphe* in February.

1942   Publication of *L'Etranger (The Stranger)* in July; leaves Algeria toward the end of 1942 to join French Resistance movement; becomes editor of clandestine newspaper *Combat*.

1942– Recurrent attacks of tuberculosis.
1944

1943   Publication of *Le Mythe de Sisyphe (The Myth of Sisyphus)*; first *Lettre à un ami allemand (Letter to a German Friend)*; becomes an editor at the Gallimard publishing house in Paris, a job he held until his death.

1944   Continues as editor of *Combat* after the Liberation; production of *Le Malentendu (The Misunderstanding)* in Paris; second *Lettre à un ami allemand;* meets Jean-Paul Sartre.

1945   Birth in Paris of the Camus twins, Catherine and Jean; production of *Caligula;* writes "Remarque sur la révolte" (point of departure for *L'Homme révolté*).

1946   Completes *La Peste;* makes lecture tour of the United States.

1947   Publication of *La Peste (The Plague)*.

1948   Trip to Algeria; production of *L'Etat de Siège (The State of Siege);* writes *Ni victimes ni bourreaux (Neither Victims nor Hangmen)*.

1950   Voyage to South America from June to August; production of *Les Justes (The Just Assassins)* in December; publication of *Actuelles I;* renewed attacks of tuberculosis from 1949–1951.

1951   Publication of *L'Homme révolté (The Rebel);* controversy with Sartre.

1952   Break with Sartre in August; working on the unfinished novel *Le Premier homme (The First Man)*, the short stories of *L'Exil et le Royaume (The Exile and the Kingdom)*, an unfinished drama *Don Juan,* and an adaptation of Dostoevski's *The Possessed*.

1953   Publication of *Actuelles II;* production of his adaptations of Calderón de la Barca's *La Devoción de la Cruz* and Pierre Larivey's *Les Esprits*.

1954   Trip to Italy in November; publication of *L'Eté*.

1955   Adaptation of *Un cas intéressant* by Dino Buzzati; trip to Greece in May; writes for Parisian newspaper *L'Express* until February, 1956.

Chronology

1956   Trip to Algeria; publication of *La Chute (The Fall);* production of his adaptation of William Faulkner's *Requiem for a Nun (Requiem pour une nonne).*

1957   Publication of *L'Exil et le Royaume (The Exile and the Kingdom)* in March; adaptation of Lope de Vega's *Chevalier d'Olmedo* in June; receives the Nobel Prize for literature in October (is the ninth and youngest Frenchman to receive it).

1958   Publication of *Actuelles III;* trip to Greece; buys home in Lourmarin.

1959   Production of his adaptation of Dostoevski's *The Possessed (Les Possédés);* appointed as director of the new state-supported experimental theater by André Malraux.

1960   January 4, killed in an automobile accident.

CHAPTER 1

The Algerian Summer

I *Camus and His Time*

TO speak of Albert Camus and his time is to separate two things that are essentially one. As an artist he could neither turn away from his time nor lose himself in it. If he had turned away from the world crisis—the breakdown of values, the struggle for power between the nations, the anxiety of the sentient man in a vast universe —he would have spoken in a void. But, conversely, insofar as he took his time as his object, he asserted his own existence as subject and could not give in to it altogether. In other words, at the very moment when he chose to share the fate of all, he asserted the individual he was. And he could not escape from this ambiguity.

The artist takes from history what he can see of it himself or undergo himself, directly or indirectly—the immediate event, in other words, and men who are alive today, not the relationship of that immediate event to a future that is invisible to the living artist.[1]

It is because Camus was aware that men are "subject to history," that he was able to speak for all in a common language that illuminated "the problems of the human conscience in our time." In 1957 his award of the Nobel Prize at the age of forty-three was not only in recognition of the excellence of his creative writing but also because of his essays which clarified the major social and political problems of his generation.[2] These essays were written concurrently with his novels and plays and in them he explored the same themes: war and resistance, executions, and exiles; the tragedies of Algeria and Hungary; the death penalty; and the role of the artist. Read along with the novels and plays, they often provide a lucid commentary on the position taken by Camus in his more widely read works.

Camus, to be understood, must be read in entirety. Just as it is impossible to understand him divorced from his time, it is impossible to grasp the impact of his thought if his works are studied independently. From his earliest writings, composed as a young, impoverished student in Mondovi, Algeria, to his final collection of short stories, written when acclaimed as one of the world's greatest authors, there is a consistent development of theme. To be convinced of the truth of this statement, one has only to read *L'Envers et l'endroit* and *Noces* in order to see that there exist in these early works evidences of deeper preoccupation.

II *Camus and Contemporary Thought*

The experiences that Camus illuminated within the four sections of *Noces* were, in many ways, in agreement with those expressed by other writers of his generation. His assumption that life was void of meaning, his apparent renunciation of hope, and his refusal of all mystical transcendence were merely an extension of the current philosophic view of the universe. He placed man in a world which is distinct from and foreign to his understanding and his desires, and he limited man's experience of this universe by inescapable death. In this way, Camus' thought moves in the same direction as that of Heidegger, Jaspers, or Sartre, but his association with these thinkers is not focused on certain systematically developed concepts. All of these men, including Camus, are concerned with the existential, but not all of them may be classified as existentialist philosophers. This point cannot be overemphasized. Camus, himself, frequently denied his alignment with existentialism; yet in spite of this denial, his critics and his reading public have continued to group him with this school. And in a certain sense Camus is an existentialist.

III *Camus' Evolving Thought*

Throughout the history of the development of Western thought, much creative thinking has been existential in its beginnings. In their attempts to evolve philosophical systems and attain universal and enduring truths, the classical philosophers all focused upon their own personal experiences and sought to understand their world and its history through these immediate experiences. Descartes' famous dictum, "I think, therefore I am," is existential in concept; yet not existential in its ontological or epistemological development. It is within this larger definition of the term "existentialist" that Camus' thought may be placed. He, like many thinkers, shared the existentialists' thesis that man exists in and is inescapably related with the world; that through his freedom of choice the individual is constantly becoming; and that death is the inevitable and final end of life. Camus, however, does not share the existentialists' tenet that human existence is void of essence. His entire thought rests on the belief in a nature common to all men. The investigation of this belief and the continual evolvement of it is the positive feature of Camus' philosophy and the link that binds one work to another.

This link from one work to the other is neither artistically unintentional nor critically imaginative. In 1951 when I asked Camus to comment upon his employment of the events of *La Malentendu* in the action of *L'Etranger* and the repetition of the action of *L'Etranger* in *La Peste,* he wrote that,

the story of *Le Malentendu* was in reality read in a newspaper. I introduced it in *L'Etranger* because I intended to develop it into a play. As you have correctly observed, the plot of *L'Etranger* similarly appears in *La Peste.* The intention there is not to be mysterious, but to indicate to the few attentive readers—at least, to my mind—my books should not be judged individually, but rather in the context of my whole work and its development.[3]

Again in 1957 in the introduction to the limited edition of *L'Envers et l'endroit,* Camus spoke of the artist's long journeying to self-knowledge that is embodied in his successive works of art.

IV   L'Envers et l'endroit

To begin at the beginning, written in 1937, *L'Envers et l'endroit* is Camus' earliest published work. The collection of five essays is a mixture of autobiography and lyrical meditation which contains no really unified argument. The title of the book itself hints at a theme which remains a suggestion rather than a logically concluded discussion. The essays present a search for some reconciliation between the "horreur de mourir" and the "jalousie de vivre." The twenty-four-year-old Camus juxtaposes the riches of the sun and sea with the misery of human poverty; to him the sensual pleasures offered by the world make death even more tragic and horrible; and the fleeting moments of tenderness and desire poignantly reveal the fact of human loneliness. Throughout the entire compact volume, each instance illustrates the contrast between happiness and suffering and the fact that these two aspects are needed to intensify each other.

The sun, sky, stars, and landscape, along with the human beings who live within these elements, are *l'envers et l'endroit* of an existence which contains both.

It was not until 1958, when Camus yielded to increasing pressure to permit a new edition of *L'Envers et l'endroit,* that the essays became well known. His own dissatisfaction with the work is easily understood from a formal point of view. The separate sections are somewhat vague and artistically weak; yet in the knowledge of Camus' later writings, these five pieces reveal his early mastery of expression and his consistent occupation with the themes of joy and despair. Later, in *Le Mythe de Sisyphe,* he turned to and emphasized the absurdity of human existence, but for the moment he focused his attention on the rapture of physical joy and wrote his manual of happiness in *Noces.*

V Noces

This second work of Camus' is again a collection of descriptive essays closely related in theme to *L'Envers et l'endroit* but more carefully worked out in their conclusion. All four of the essays are set in the Mediterranean world whose images never ceased to influence both the literary and the philosophical writings of Camus. These images of the sun, the sea, Florence, and Algiers remain easily recognizable entities; but in Camus' handling of them, they become charged with a complex, intense suggestiveness and play a fixed role in what soon becomes recognizable as his instinctively felt and expressed inner world.

"Noces à Tipasa," the first essay, portrays the total surrender of self to the eternal beauty of the universe. The momentary correspondence between man and nature is expressed by an exalted lyrical description of the sensual delights experienced at the Roman ruins near the ancient North African village. Surrounded by lush vegetation, intoxicated by the perfumes of exotic flowers, drenched by the sun, and enchanted by the silver and white of the sea and the flaxen-blue of the sky, he feels the ecstasy of life and his own harmony with the earth. He says,

Toward evening I felt a strange joy, that joy which actors know when they have played their role well. They feel in the most precise sense, that they have made their gestures coincide with those of the ideal personage they are representing; that they have participated, in some way, in a design made in advance, and which they have made come alive and beat with their own heart. That is precisely what I felt. I had played my role well. (24)

From the rhapsodic nuptials between man and the universe, the mood of enchantment is quickly broken in "Le Vent à Djémila." In the wind-swept ruins on the plateau of Djémila, he discovers his identity with the solitude and silence of the dead city, and he learns to accept a death without hope. He writes, "I do not like to believe that death opens onto another life. For me it is a closed door" (35). It is here in Djémila that he obstinately refuses all the future promises of the world and clings to the richness of the present: "Everything that is proposed to me endeavors to take away from man the weight of his own life. And . . . it is exactly this certain weight of life that I demand and receive" (35).

"L'Eté à Alger," the third essay, is concerned with the physical beauties of Algiers and its people "without religion and without idols" (60). This is a race without a past, without tradition, wholly cast in its present. Everything it does shows a horror of stability and a disregard for the future. In the harsh summer sky of Algiers, before which all truths can be uttered, and in the violent and keen face of this race, Camus finds "nothing on which to hang a mythology, a literature, an ethic, or a religion, but stones, flesh, stars, and those truths the hand can touch" (65). "Everything here suggests the horror of dying in a country that invites one to live" (63). In the midst of the sensual delight brought about by the union of man with earth, Camus is aware that "everything that exalts life at the same time increases its absurdity" (67).

In the final essay, "Le Désert," Camus writes, "I admire, I admire that bond which, in the world, unites mankind, that double reflection in which my heart can intervene and dictate its happiness to the precise bounds where the world can then complete or destroy it" (102). It is in Italy in the "desert magnificent to the heart" that Camus meditates upon his conception of a happiness that affirms the dignity and value of human life in a world that remains indifferent to man's desires. "And what more legitimate accord can unite man to life than the double consciousness of his desire for duration and his destiny of death? In this way one at least learns to count on nothing and consider the present as the only truth given us by grace" (94). It is this concluding essay of *Noces*, "Le Désert," that reinforces the central theme of the entire collection: that although life ends in death and there is no transcendence, there remains the possibility of man's attainment of a special kind of happiness.

VI *The Constants of Camus' Art*

Although carefully selected and more clearly defined in his later writings, the constants of Camus' art and thought are already discernible in *L'Envers et l'endroit* and *Noces*. First, the titles chosen are in themselves indicative of a technique that Camus employed throughout his artistic career. They, along with *L'Etranger, La Peste, La Chute, L'Exil et le Royaume,* attract the reader's attention and compel him to expand these titles into all-encompassing symbols for the works. *L'Envers et l'endroit* suggests a duality that is perhaps more clearly spelled out in *L'Exil et le Royaume; Noces* is the marriage of these two aspects of existence, whereas *L'Etranger* is out of tune with his world; *La Peste* introduces disease and corruption within the kingdom, and *La Chute* indicates a complete severance— a fall from the state of grace. Secondly, the poetic luxuriance of the language employed by Camus in these early essays remains an essential aspect of his later writings. Although *L'Envers et l'endroit* and *Noces* are intensely lyrical, Camus places a restraint upon his writing that permits a fusion of image and thought and blends emotion and reason in a highly successful manner. The lyrical expression of an attitude toward life later evolves into an intellectual investigation of the same attitude, but the lyrical aspect is never totally absent from Camus' writing.

The sentiment of absurdity that is later given its distinct form in *Le Mythe de Sisyphe* as "the divorce between man and his life, between the actor and his setting" (18)[4] is investigated on a personal level in these early essays. In the very moment of his enjoyment of the sensual delights of the natural world, Camus is aware of the tragic implications of that moment; for by definition the intensity of the experience cannot endure. Man is born and man dies, and between these two knowns, man must discover the "present riches." The exaltation of the natural world and the complete refusal of the "later on" that are expressed in *Noces* form the core of Camus' thought. The fleeting pleasures of the warmth of the sun, the joys of swimming, the tranquillity of the cool Mediterranean evenings that give man a precious feeling of communion with the world are contrasted with the immortality and indifference of nature. The Algerian summers will succeed one another in an unending procession; and although mankind's enjoyment of these summers may also infinitely endure, the tragic fact remains that each individual's enjoyment is limited in time. The truth of human transience as opposed to the desire for permanence is one of the major philosophical themes underlying *Noces*. *Noces* is Camus' manual of happiness, and the intensity of the physical joy it describes increases the awareness of the absurd.

The problem raised by the acutely personal atheism developed in these early essays is a question of a dual truth. On an abstract philosophical level there is the fact of man's desire for life as opposed to the inevitability of his death, but on an uncomplicated personal level there is the overwhelming earthly happiness found within this tragic framework. In "Le Désert," the final essay of *Noces*, Camus describes how he wandered in the cloisters of Santissima Annunziata and read the inscriptions to the dead. As night was falling, he sat at the foot of a pillar and alone,

was like someone seized by the throat, who shouts out his faith as if it were his dying words. Everything in me protested against such a resignation. "You must accept," said the tombstones. No, and I was right to rebel. I must follow this joy that goes indifferent and absorbed as a pilgrim upon the earth, must follow it step by step. (88–89)

Although the tombs told him that his revolt was meaningless and that he must acquiesce to death, for Camus, this answer had no relevance. To him, what was real was experienced; and in his revolt, in his refusal of sin, and in his rejection of eternal life, he gained a greater intensity of life and a possibility of happiness.

By refusing to accept the religious consolation and solution to man's mortality, Camus renounced hope in the usual sense of the word. However, he did not accept the equation of refusal and resignation. "To live is not to be resigned" (69). Camus asked that man, in his conscious certainty of a death without hope, refuse the world but not renounce it. To accept the transience of life rather than renounce it in favor of eternal salvation is to refuse resignation. Camus reflected upon hope and man's defenselessness before death in "L'Eté à Alger":

From Pandora's box, where swarmed the evils of humanity, the Greeks left out hope after all the rest as the most terrible of all. I do not know of a more moving symbol. For hope, contrary to what is believed, is equivalent to resignation. And to live is not to be resigned. (69)

Camus' renouncement of hope does not negate the possibility of happiness. Happiness results from man's oneness with his universe. The individual accepts his mortal destiny and attains a happiness which is the affirmation of the dignity and unique value of human existence. Within the closing pages of *Noces*, Camus has presented another crucial point in his thinking. The happiness that is held forth to man is as brief and as fleeting as life itself; yet he asks "What have I to do with imperishable truth, even were I to desire such a thing? It is not made to my measure. To desire it would be to deceive myself" (100).

It is only after concluding the entire collection that the seemingly pessimistic opening quotation taken from Stendhal's *Chroniques italiennes* becomes significant. "The executioner strangled Cardinal Carrafa with a silk cord which broke: twice he had to try again. The Cardinal watched the executioner without deigning to utter a word." The description of this brief encounter between the Cardinal and his executioner illustrates the central point of the essays. Man, like the Cardinal, knows his fate; but also like the Cardinal, in full knowledge of his inevitable death, he does not cry out in futile lamentation.

VII *The End of His Algerian Summer*

Camus never again knew the complete harmony with the world that he expressed in *Noces*. With the advent of World War II, his Algerian summer ended; and in place of his natural gods of the sun, the sea, and the night, he was forced into the world of barbed-wire fences, tyranny, and war.[5] In September, 1939, Pascal Pia appointed him editor-in-chief of *Le Soir Republicain;* and after this paper was forced to close in January, 1940, because of violation of censorship regulations, Pia was instrumental in securing a position for him as rewrite man for the *Paris-Soir*. In Paris, Camus gained the experience that prepared him for the editing and disseminating of the clandestine newspaper *Combat* during the Nazi occupation of France. It was also in Paris that he was introduced to the prevalent intellectual atmosphere of France. Sartre's insistence that a writer could no longer avoid the moral responsibility for acts and attitudes inspired by his books was in accord with Camus' own belief that the artist is obliged to bear witness to man's basic right to freedom and justice in the face of history.

In his preface to the 1959 edition of Jean Grenier's *Les Iles*, Camus wrote that it was Grenier who showed him, that the light and the splendor of bodies were beautiful, but that they would perish and that we must therefore love them with the urgency of despair. Perhaps this was the only way of guiding a young man brought up outside traditional religions towards a deeper way of thinking. . . . I needed to be reminded of mysterious and sacred things, of the finite nature of man, of a love that was impossible, in order that I might one day return to my natural gods with less arrogance. Thus I owe Grenier . . . a debt that will never end.[6]

Although according to Camus' admission, it was Grenier who turned him from an unreflective enjoyment of life to the constant meditation on the human condition which permeates his entire work, it was Paris of the war years and the success which was accorded him there after the publication of *L'Etranger* late in 1942 and *Le Mythe de Sisyphe* early in 1943 that imposed upon him the position as prophet and director of conscience to the younger generation. With his triumph as a literary figure came the end of Camus' Algerian summer, but the constants in his art and thought are born of his early life in North Africa.

CHAPTER 2

Man and the Absurd

I *Publication of* L'Etranger *and* Le Mythe de Sisyphe

L'ETRANGER and *Le Mythe de Sisyphe* are without question the most often discussed of Camus' works. This popularity is readily understood, for these two books corresponded to the atmosphere that permeated Nazi-occupied France at the date of their publication and have continued to dominate the mood of the post-war Western world up until the present time. With the daily threat to humanity that existed amid the European disaster of the 1940's, it was difficult to believe in eternal values or naive optimism, and human life became a consciously more precise thing. In this time when no one could afford just to exist passively, Camus' fictive portrayal and philosophical account of the absurd hero seemed to express the uncertainty of the war-conscious Europeans; and Camus, along with Sartre, became the voice of an anxiety-ridden people. The reason for the continuation of the books' popularity into our own time needs no further comment than that implied by the horrifying news presented to us hourly by radio, television, and the newspapers.

As is often true with books that receive immediate critical and popular acclaim, the public misunderstood the author's total intention in these works. Following the books' publication, the identification of Camus with the absurd heroes of *L'Etranger* and *Le Mythe de Sisyphe* created a problem for the author that persisted for several years. Given the time in which they appeared on the literary scene, it was perhaps inevitable that the call to happiness—the positive side of Camus' work—should have been ignored. Understandably, the appeal of his writing was mainly derived from the description of the incoherent world that his mind experienced, but this aspect was only one facet of his purpose. His aim from the beginning was to examine and not to proffer the philosophy of the absurd. In 1950, Camus was sufficiently distressed by his identification as a philoso-

Man and the Absurd

pher of the absurd to write in "L'Enigme" that his primary concern in *Le Mythe de Sisyphe* was to examine the logical basis and intellectual justification of the "absurd sensibility" as he found it expressed in contemporary philosophy. As late as 1955, for the American edition of *Le Mythe de Sisyphe*, Camus again asserted that this essay marked for him "the beginning of an idea." Indeed, both of these statements are a repetition of a brief introductory remark for the original publication of the essay in which Camus succinctly wrote that his purpose was to "deal with an absurd sensitivity . . . and not with an absurd philosophy."

II *Relation of* Le Mythe *to Camus' Other Writings*

We are again, then, dealing with a personal development of an idea. Unlike Sartre, Camus was not a professionally trained philosopher and he spoke more as an involved individual than as an objective metaphysician. Following as it does *L'Envers et l'endroit* and *Noces*, *Le Mythe de Sisyphe* may be read as an expansion of an emotional experience in a more rational and philosophical manner. The idea of personal happiness that Camus had discovered through his acceptance of both the physical joys and the transience of existence that concluded *Noces* is now analyzed in its broader implications. In *Noces*, Camus found that all his "idols have feet of clay" (102); in *Le Mythe de Sisyphe*, he no longer searches for "gods of light and idols of mud" but feels a need "to find the middle path leading to the faces of man" (103).

It is this emotionally felt need that leads Camus to an exploration of man and his manifold problems. The intellectual malady brought about by the contradiction between thought and experience, mind and feelings, intentions and possibilities—universally experienced by thinking men—gives rise to an emotionally understandable search for a reason for living. The essay begins with a consideration of the one truly serious problem of "judging whether life is or is not worth living." According to Camus, the answer man gives involves "the fundamental question of philosophy" (3). At the outset of his investigation, the learned and classical dialectic is sacrificed to a more modest attitude of mind based upon common sense and understanding—upon the relationship between individual thought and suicide. Characteristic of Camus, man's understanding of the world involves the reduction of that world to the human; for a world that can be explained even with bad reasons is a familiar world and one in which man can survive. It is at the moment that he becomes divorced from his life and feels himself an alien in a universe divested of illusion and light that the question of suicide arises, and it is at this moment that his awareness of the feeling of the absurd begins.

III *The Feeling of Absurdity*

In his attempt to define this feeling of absurdity, Camus enumerates the various ways in which the absurd manifests itself. In certain situations, when asked what one is thinking, it is not unusual to become suddenly aware of an "odd state of soul . . . in which the chain of daily gestures is broken, in which the heart vainly seeks the link that will connect it again" (12). Just as this experience may give rise to the absurd feeling, so too is it possible, for no specified reason, that in the midst of the normal monotony of the Monday through Saturday, workaday world, one stops and questions the meaning of his routine and "everything begins in that weariness tinged with amazement" (13). Camus emphasizes the importance of the word "begins," for the weariness which results from the acts of a mechanical life may inaugurate the impulse of consciousness which impels each of us to think of himself in relationship to time; and once having acknowledged this place in time, the logical thought process leads us to the fact of death—the most overpowering evidence of the absurd.

IV *Intellectual Basis for the Absurd*

Aware of the emotional manifestations of the absurd, Camus searches for an intellectual basis for his feeling. Through a brief investigation of the history of science, he learns that scientific truth can only explain the world through the enumeration of phenomena. The mind can neither explain nor understand the universe or even the individual through whom it operates. In psychology, as in logic, there are truths but no truth. Since the beginnings of time the human mind has longed for a real and rational explanation of the world, but it is forced to admit that no such explanation can be given. All the knowledge on earth gives man nothing to assure him that the world is his.

V *The Truth of Absurdity*

Through the emotional and intellectual awareness of the fact of death in contrast to the potent desire for immortality, Camus derives the truth of absurdity. In simple terminology, the absurd always involves a contradiction between two things. Here that contradiction exists between man's longing for duration and the inevitability of his death. It is the confrontation between the desire and the reality —neither the one nor the other in itself—that is the absurd.

. . . the feeling of the absurd becomes clear and definite. I said that the world is absurd, but I was too hasty. This world in itself is not reasonable, that is all that can be said. But what is absurd is the confrontation of this irrational and the wild longing for clarity whose call echoes in the human heart. The absurd depends as much on man as on the world. (21)

For the moment, then, we experience the absurd as the unique and vital link between man and the world. And through the absurd we know what man desires, what the world offers, and what unites man and the world.

VI *Limitations of Past Philosophies of the Absurd*

From the recognition of the truth of the absurd as the result of the clash between our demand for an explanation and the mysterious evasiveness of existence, it is necessary for Camus to ascertain if thought is possible under these conditions. He turns to the writings of Heidegger, Jaspers, Shestov, Kierkegaard and Husserl, and in them he finds a common recognition of an absurd universe and a basic relationship of mind. However, once faced with the absurd, none of these philosophers had been true to it. All of them eventually destroy it by deifying the contradiction between human need and the unreasonable silence of the world and take the unjustifiable leap into an irrational explanation that resolves the antinomy between man and the world. In every case this explanation is forced and of a religious nature. Whatever the method, the religious philosopher proffers a solution which by its rational incomprehensibility is beyond the reach of human reason. According to Camus, for the absurd mind there is nothing beyond reason; therefore the attitude of these men which tends toward the eternal unjustly dismisses the absurd and alters the nature of the problem. The absurd cannot be transcended, for it requires no other universe than our daily world, our earth, our fellow human beings and ourselves. By its very nature, the mystical-religious interpretation of the philosophers under discussion has neither met nor solved the question raised by the absurd. The acceptance of their ideas, in its retreat before what the mind has brought to light, constitutes philosophical suicide.

As has been suggested already, Camus' search for truth involves a personal need to understand the world, to find a unity in it that can form the basis for a meaningful life. He discovers through investigation of historical and contemporary philosophical thought that the unity which he so desperately desires can only be brought about if the affirmer of it makes his judgment from a position outside of it. Once he moves outside the unity, he affirms an exception to it and ends in contradiction. Neither the deification of the absurd by Jaspers and Kierkegaard, nor Shestov's identification of it with God, answers Camus' immediate need to explain the contradiction between his desire for clarity and unity and the world's irrationality, disunity, and fragmentation. Camus accepts the truth of the absurd and maintains that he must follow this truth in all its consequences.

VII   The Burden of the Absurd

Since he cannot remain faithful to the absurd by an escape through the philosophical leap, he is forced to take upon himself the burden of the absurd in which he learns not to hope and in which he remains in continual revolt against the world. Revolt is the first of three consequences to total acceptance of the absurd. It is a constant confrontation between man and his obscurity, an ongoing struggle with the absurd. It challenges the world every moment and it extends awareness to the whole of experience. "It is that constant presence of man in his own eyes. It is not aspiration, for it is devoid of hope" (54). Revolt gives life its value and its majesty, for it creates the beauty of the human mind at grips with a reality which exceeds it.

The second consequence of the absurd is freedom. It is not the usual conception of freedom as something given by God or some higher being. Through the privation of hope and future which the absurd implies, the individual is granted an infinitely greater freedom of action. He no longer is concerned with the "somedays" of the future, for death is there as the only reality. In the absurd revelation, the ordinary man realizes that insofar as he had planned his life on the basis of the future, he was conforming to given goals which seemed to be a part of a non-existent larger meaning. The absurd, however, in its denial of a future, offers him a deeper independence and a freedom which the human heart can experience and live.

The absurd man thus catches sight of a burning and frigid, transparent and limited universe in which nothing is possible but everything is given, and beyond which all is collapse and nothingness. He can then decide to accept such a universe and draw from it his strength, his refusal to hope, and the unyielding evidence of a life without consolation. (60)

The third consequence of the absurd is a passion to exhaust that which is provided by the present moment. In an absurd universe each moment assumes a precious quality, for man is aware of his approaching death. "The present and the succession of presents before an ever conscious mind, this is the ideal of the absurd man" (63–64). Man must be conscious of each of his experiences, for only through his awareness can he live to the maximum.

As a result of his search for truth in a world that offers no hope and no illusions, Camus has derived the three consequences of revolt, freedom, and passion. Through the activity of his consciousness he has transformed the invitation to death that opened the essay into a rule of life, and he has demonstrated the incomprehensibility of human life in order to refute the senseless conclusion that it is therefore meaningless.

Hitherto, and it has not been wasted effort, people have played on words and pretended to believe that refusing to grant a meaning to life necessarily leads to declaring that it is not worth living. In truth, there is no necessary common measure between these two judgments. (8)

The value of life is enhanced by the awareness of the impossibility of reducing it to human understanding, and in the pages that follow, Camus portrays examples of the absurd man who has accepted the conclusions of his argument.

VIII   *Four Examples of the Absurd Man*

Through his choice of the seducer, the actor, the conqueror, and the artist, Camus limits himself to men who by the nature of their lives illustrate the "passion to exhaust everything that is given." In his description of these four men, he presents each of them as being conscious of the fact that his activity is useless. Neither the Don Juan, who receives the same joy from each new woman he seduces, nor the actor, who shares the life of each character he portrays, nor the conqueror, who acts from fascination, nor the artist (the most absurd of all) who creates has any illusions about a life hereafter. Each seeks momentary happiness and nothing further; there is no attempt or hope to solve the problems of human existence. And it is this honesty toward life, this consciousness of the uselessness of their lives that has given them their freedom and their happiness. "Outside of that simple fatality of death, everything, joy or happiness, is liberty. A world remains of which man is the sole master" (117). In this world existence is of infinite value because it is finite in time. It is a world without God in which destiny is a human affair and in which consciousness of this fact is an invitation to happiness.

IX *Sisyphus*

In the concluding passage of *Le Mythe de Sisyphe*, Sisyphus is seen as the incarnation of the absurd hero. Sisyphus, like the absurd men, hated death and the gods and was passionately attached to life. According to legend, he, the favored of mortals, was accused of a certain levity in regard to the gods and as a result of his actions was condemned to Hades. Later he obtained Pluto's permission to return briefly to earth in order to chastise his wife for having cast his unburied body into the middle of the public square, but once again among the sun, the warm stones, and the sea of the world, he no longer wished to return to Hades. So enraged were the gods that they sent Mercury to lead Sisyphus back to the underworld. For eternity he was condemned to roll a boulder up to the crest of a mountain from which it would crash back to the bottom.

It is the moment in which Sisyphus watches the stone roll down the mountainside that interests Camus. It is during that return downward to resume his torment that Camus imagines Sisyphus to have his hour of consciousness. It is a consciousness of the extent of his own misery; of the recognition of his eternal destiny. However, in this moment of recognition, Sisyphus transforms his torment into his victory, for he realizes that he is without hope and without power. Through his lucid insight into the truth, he becomes superior to his destiny, for he has seen it for what it is and has become his own master. At that subtle instant when Sisyphus returns toward his rock, he contemplates the series of unrelated actions which become his fate, created by him, combined in his memory and to be sealed by his death. Convinced of the wholly human origin of all that is human, Camus goes on:

I leave Sisyphus at the foot of the mountain. One always finds one's burden again. But Sisyphus teaches the higher fidelity that negates the gods and raises rocks. He too concludes that all is well. This universe henceforth without a master seems to him neither sterile nor futile. Each atom of that stone, each mineral flake of that night-filled mountain, in itself forms a world. The struggle itself toward the heights is enough to fill a man's heart. One must imagine Sisyphus happy. (123)

The essay is concluded with this optimistic portrayal of Sisyphus. Void of hope, he nevertheless finds life so fully satisfying that he is content to spend it in his eternal struggle to the heights. Through his consciousness of the world without appeal, he has discovered a happiness which springs from despair, and he has learned that the most appalling truths lose their power once they are recognized and accepted. The attitude illustrated by Sisyphus is alien to any possible form of physical or philosophical suicide.

X Evaluation

The ideas of *Le Mythe de Sisyphe* are the momentary result of an ever-evolving attempt on Camus' part to understand the complex realities of human experience; and at this point in his development, the absurdist doctrine has been carried to its limits. The passive estrangement which man suffers in the face of the absurd will later be expanded and transformed into a new line of reasoning, but for now all we know is that our world is without God or fixed values. These ideas will be tested in the later creative works in an attempt to discover whether or not human dignity can persist in a world of unlimited freedom, and the development of the absurd experiment will explore more intently an essential dimension of human experience which opposes and supersedes the absurd. This dimension which Camus labels revolt is already defined in a limited sense in *Le Mythe de Sisyphe* as man's rebellion against a world which denies his need for unity and coherence, but the reader of this essay is left with a vague and unsatisfactory meaning of this term.

To a degree, Camus' experiment in *Le Mythe de Sisyphe* is but another in a long line of similar processes. The experience of the absurd is certainly not peculiar either to Camus or to twentieth-century reasoning. Nietzsche, of course, poetically provided the classical formulation of the Death-of-God theme, but as early as 1822 Hegel had gravely spoken of the infinite pain of God's absence; and such comments as Gide's "I am convinced that God is not," or Valéry's "Man thinks, therefore I am, says the Universe," or Flaubert's "Suppose the absurd were true?" all point to a historical development of the idea of a humanity trying to learn to do without God. What makes Camus unusual is the fact that this book is an experiment and not an unqualified attitude or philosophical position.

This type of experimental philosophy is unprecedented and emphasizes the importance which Camus places on the idea of development. He cannot, or at least does not, proceed through induction to construct a consistent interpretive scheme of the universe, but rather progresses through personal involvement with the universe to an understanding of it that is acceptable in human terminology. It is the human element that consistently enters into Camus' thought that prohibits any possibility of a strictly systematic approach to any one individual piece of writing. It might be said that Camus thinks aloud through his writings, and just as thought is a constantly-evolving process, so too is his experimental philosophizing.

Again, the necessity of reading him in his entirety cannot be overemphasized. A purely literary approach to his work is almost impossible, for so many of his ideas are clarified in his philosophical writings. On the other hand, a philosophical approach is also unsatisfactory because in his particular thought process, the abstract philosophical ideas must be translated into human situations before they are completely meaningful. By combining the excellence of his imagination and the magnificence of his style, he is able to objectify philosophical theories through a fictional situation. Although to many critics, following the lead of Sartre's explication of *L'Etranger*, the meaning of the novel becomes clarified through the understanding of *Le Mythe de Sisyphe*, the reverse process is also a valid one, for it is through the actions of Meursault that the philosophical ideas contained in this essay take on vitality and significance for the average man caught in the torment of the twentieth century.

CHAPTER 3

Abstract Man

I *Reception of* L'Etranger

CAMUS' *L'Etranger* has taken its rightful place alongside the works of Faulkner, Joyce, Kafka, and Dostoevski on the bookshelves of most American college students. Because of the beauty and simplicity of its language, it is often chosen by professors of French in introductory courses, and once in the hands of inquiring students, the power and the enigmatic nature of the book suddenly become stimulants to further thought. Although *L'Etranger* may serve as the student's initiation to philosophical concepts that he does not fully comprehend, this story of a man who is executed for having smoked at his mother's wake arouses his intellectual curiosity and leads him into a never-ending questioning of the meaning of life. For the American student, Camus makes an indispensable contribution to the understanding of himself and the conflicts of his time.

Barring the overwrought eulogies, the unquestionable popularity that *L'Etranger* has enjoyed during the past twenty-five years is valid proof of its significance. The book was published in 1942 when Camus was twenty-nine, but since it actually belongs more to the emotional and intellectual climate of his earlier years, this fact may in part account for its appeal to the present generation. Like many young Americans today, the Camus of Algiers had experienced neither the ravages of a war nor the sophisticated climate of a large, European city, but he was acutely aware of the newness and originality of his country and of the strange and fascinating beauty of this world. It was his intense concern with ethical values and his intellectual need to establish a valid justification for life that led him to a career as a writer, and it was his ability to express his thoughts artistically that led to the early acceptance of Camus as one of Europe's greatest authors.

II *Meursault*

L'Etranger is the first internationally successful writing to emerge from this period of Camus' life, and its popularity is in no small measure closely related to the fact that Meursault's problems are essentially those of most young men in a predominantly bourgeois, Christian society.[1] Meursault's story, related in the first person, must be that of a young man, for it is only valid in youth to refuse to conform to the rules of life as they are dictated by society. Once youth has passed, the rules of the game are not easily forgotten. As we learn to know Meursault's character, we are tempted to see him as irresponsible and anti-social. He acts in a human situation as though human relationships do not exist. It is a fact that he becomes enmeshed in a sordid affair involving Raymond without ever questioning the possible outcome, and it is also a fact that he murders an Arab. We are led to believe that he is completely indifferent to everything except physical sensations. He is thirty and a bachelor. He dutifully pursues his profession as a clerk, but he is more interested in the pleasant dryness of a towel in the washroom at midday and its clamminess at night than he is in a possible promotion to Paris. He lives in a succession of presents in which all pleasures are sensual experiences. Smoking, eating, swimming, fornication are all equal acts. Even the death of his mother has no immediate effect upon him. He is detached from any of the entanglements that generally surround human existence, and he remains so detached until after his murder of the Arab.

This development of Meursault's initial unawareness to an almost alarming awareness after the murder would be inconceivable if we did not also catch a glimpse of another Meursault who lived as a student in Paris and was presumably not always so passive as we find him in the first part of the book. Actually, he is far from being totally deprived of passion, for it is his passion which leads him to his decision to be honest to himself and to base his life on the truth of being and feeling. And it is this decision that makes him a stranger in a society whose existence depends upon everyone's concession to its codes and rituals.

III *The Dominant Theme*

It is in the second part of the book that the dominant theme is made clear to the reader. The murder of the Arab is the event that binds together the discontinuous succession of moments of Meursault's earlier life to form a past which can be judged. Confined in prison and condemned to death, Meursault is forced to evaluate his relationship with the world. He is aware that society refused him the final rights of judgment and denied him his importance as an individual. He knows that the absolute religious and social values by which he was judged are conventional and outworn. He is cognizant of all these things; yet, in full realization of the limitations of society, his final wish is not to withdraw from it but to resubject himself to the tortuous entanglements of day-to-day living. The reason for this wish can only be explained by the one additional discovery made by him. Near death, he has learned that life with all its inexplicable involvements is not only worth living, but that it offers man his one chance for happiness. The absurdity of life, which actually has nothing to do with either society or man's behavior within society, cannot be denied or eradicated. It is in reality an invitation to a happiness completely rooted in the knowledge that men live and men die. Meursault's ". . . I, too, felt ready to start life all over again" (154)[2] echoes Sisyphus' thought, "The struggle itself toward the heights is enough to fill a man's heart" (123).

The fight toward the summit for Meursault demands almost superhuman endurance, for his discovery of the singular value of life does not occur until the last pages of the novel. He is dragged through defeat after defeat before he is able to acknowledge the one glaring truth that he chose to ignore throughout the major portion of the novel. In this way *L'Etranger* is a novel of development in which the protagonist must go through the agonizing experience of affirming that the infinite value of life lies in the very finiteness of its nature. For Meursault, the existence which he had been leading is brought into question; he rejects the rational explanation of man's position proffered by the law and the complexities of day-to-day living; he rejects suicide and affirms the value of life; finally, as a consequence of his failure to surmount or eradicate the finiteness of existence, he recognizes the absurdity of life, and the potentiality of man gains new dignity through this recognition.

From the moment of Meursault's arrest, the world in terms of his experience becomes inexplicable to him. According to standards by which he had conducted his life, there is no basis for his arrest. He had based his actions upon complete indifference to everything except physical sensations; and projecting this philosophy to the extreme, he saw no difference between firing and not firing the shots into the body of the Arab. With his arrest, he is abruptly introduced into a world that is inexplicable in the terms of his understanding.

The moment of the clash between the opposed demands of his individual moral code and the social code by which he is judged initiates his gradual awakening to the absurdity of the universe.

Before Meursault acknowledges the unauthenticity of his own existence, he endeavors to strike out against the society which has placed him in confinement. In agreement with his way of life, he does not actively seek explanation for his arrest; however, by being placed in confinement, he is automatically exposed to a set of values devised by the law courts and the church. Neither of these social agencies is able to resolve his conflict; but since they are responsible for his condemnation, they are the instruments which lead him to a positive affirmation of the value of life. In his quest for some meaning to life, it is at the moment of imminent death that he finally turns from exterior forces inward to himself. Although he chose to transform the world rather than conform to it, he dies knowing that he has failed. Throughout his life, he refused to question anything. Hoping to transform the world by ignoring its limitations, he accepted only the sensual aspects of life. At the time of his death he realizes for the first time that happiness cannot exist in a world where all actions are equal. He discovers in death that in the face of the absurd fact that all men must die, no one can afford just to exist. To fail to question the meaning of life is to condemn the individual and the world to nothingness.

IV *The Affirmation of Life*

In *L'Etranger*, Meursault is, above all else, a man who wants to go on living. No matter how unbearable prison life becomes for him, death is never a temptation. Life at any price is worth the living. His desire for life is most clearly expressed when he says, "I've often thought that had I been compelled to live in the trunk of a dead tree, with nothing to do but gaze up at the patch of sky just overhead, I'd have got used to it by degrees" (95). He is an everyday man—an office clerk—who is suddenly interrupted in the hopes and ambitions of an ordinary life and brought to a painful realization that death is an inescapable fact. In his day-to-day living, his personal relationship with the world had not been brought into question. In his thorough enjoyment of each sensual pleasure, he had never thought of the time when these experiences would be ended by death. It is at the moment of arrest that he is jarred out of his feeling of complacency and is forced to think of himself in association with the world. That he cannot immediately accept the nature of the relationship between man and the universe is explicable in the terms of the false social order to which he is subjected. The feeling of absurdity that arises from the clash of the desire of the human mind that the world should be explicable in human terms and the fact that the world is not thus understandable becomes present in Meursault's thoughts throughout *L'Etranger*, but the absurdity of the universe is not unconditionally accepted by him until the last pages of the narrative. He, as a representative of everyman, must seek out, be subjected to, and finally reject all the time-honored answers offered to solve man's enigmatic relationship to his universe. In his search for a meaning to life, the one positive conclusion that Meursault finally comes to is that life is finite. Nowhere within this world can he find any proof of a life beyond the grave. He knows that he exists and that the world exists, and he becomes increasingly aware that anything beyond these two tangible facts is mere construction. He tosses about from the purely sensual to the logical to the religious, but nowhere is he able to find anything but paradox. Every new adventure reinforces the illogic of the earth. Meursault discovers but one truth concerning human existence: "A childishly simple, obvious, almost silly truth, but one that's hard to come by and heavy to endure. . . . Men die and they are not happy" (I, 8).[3] Meursault's search for truth, unity, and a meaning to life is constantly blocked by the irrational world. Finally faced with imminent death, exhausted by a fruitless battle waged in an attempt to alter the unalterable, he is forced to accept the doctrine of absurdity. He relinquishes all efforts to transcend or destroy the limitations of human existence and submits to an indifferent nature that remains forever distinct from and foreign to the nature of man.

In *L'Etranger* the acceptance of the doctrine of the absurd in no way implies disdain of the universe. Throughout the novel Meursault clings to the strange, fascinating beauty of a world that he cannot comprehend. The warmth of a female body, the odors of the sea, the brilliance of the sun are, in fact, those things which make life worth living for him. Rather than a rejection of the universe, Meursault's desire for life is deeply rooted in a total acceptance of the natural universe. What he learns through his contacts with the superimposed structures of false society is that man is alone and that all his actions are equally unimportant and insignificant in their effect upon the nature of the universe. All men must die, and Meursault realizes that nothing can be done to alter the course of human existence. He finally ceases searching for some possible escape from his human fate and totally resigns himself to the grandeur of the universe. He cannot understand the relationship between man and the world, but somehow he no longer needs to understand it.

In addition he realizes through his contacts during confinement that all men are oppressed by external values which have nothing to do with either the nature of man or the nature of the universe. Man's life is ruled by outdated pretensions which should, as the men who created them, be disintegrated into ashes. Meursault's recognition of the fact that the oppression of man is something he can act upon is the beginning of his revolt. Although this feeling of revolt comes too late to have any positive results in his life, it is clearly formulated. By implication, in Meursault's wish that he be greeted by howls of execration at his execution, an invitation is offered to mankind for a life freed from involvement in the outworn dictates of twentieth-century civilization. Through Meursault's failure as an individual, he offers positive hope to the rest of mankind. His entire existence was squandered in a quest for a meaning to life that he finally discovered near the time of his death. However, this waste of human effort was not only his fault but also that of an outworn social code which made no provisions for the deviations in man's actions. The invitation offered by Meursault to all men is that they cease their attempt to conquer the unconquerable, that they acknowledge the absurdity of life, and that in full recognition of the limitations placed upon mankind they seek to build a new society that once again acknowledges the dignity of man above all else.

The implication underlying the theme of *L'Etranger* is that a world in which God is dead and destiny is a human affair need not be an unhappy world. From the individual recognition of the absurdity of life emerges a happiness which is neither sensual nor transcendent, but which is the affirmation of the dignity and unique value of human life. In a world which offers no hope to mankind, man learns through the double consciousness of his desire for duration and his destiny of death to count on nothing and to consider the present as the only truth given to him. From the consciousness that he is his own end and the only end to which he can aspire, it is right for man to question, but this questioning must result in an affirmation of the world of true values.

Camus' basic attack is directed against the unnecessary suffering entailed by man in his relationships with his fellow man. He pleads for recognition of the tragic journey of life and for recognition on the part of man that he is not an isolated being. He is appalled by man's blindness not only in refusing to recognize the tragedy of human life but also in refusing to see the value of acting decently upon it. Man's questioning alone leads him to frustration and resultant pessimism, but this pessimism must be a point of departure which takes him out of his individual despair to the recognition that the transitoriness of life is the link of solidarity he has with all mankind. Once he is aware that he does not have to battle alone, he can combine his force with that of all other men to reestablish human dignity.

All Meursault's actions highlight the major tragedy of the twentieth century. In man's failure to question himself, he denies the one thing that could restore his human dignity. Frustrated and bored by the external aspects of the world that crushes him, without once realizing that he is a member of the only species that can express its frustration and boredom in words, he must not conform to or ignore these aspects. The sacrifice of Meursault to a society which attempted to repress his individuality is Camus' plea to mankind that it recognize and alleviate the tragedy of the twentieth century. The man who fails to question himself is dead while he yet lives. The hope that Camus offers is that the individual invest his energies in the betterment of the one positive fact to which he can cling: his life on this earth, in this moment.

V   *Relationship of* L'Etranger *to Camus' Other Works*

It is also the character of Meursault that most clearly illustrates the continual development of Camus' thoughts on the absurd. Meursault not only recalls the world of *L'Envers et l'endroit* and *Noces,* but he prepares the reader for new extensions of the absurdist experiment that are analyzed in Camus' later writings. Meursault's instinctive awareness of the increased value of life brought about by the fact of mortality and his enjoyment of physical sensations recall Camus' expression of his feelings at Djémila when he said, "If I obstinately refuse all the 'later on' of this world, it is because I do not want to give up my present riches." The warmth of the sun, the cry of the boys selling iced drinks in the square, the pleasures of the beach, the cool Mediterranean evenings are the joys that Meursault sorely misses as he lies in his prison cell, and these are the same experiences that Camus describes in *Noces* as the source of a happy life. Meursault as the man who cannot lie possesses the one moral quality which Camus most admired in his fellow Algerians. In the simple pagan civilization of North Africa, men observed certain basic rules in their relationships with one another. This feeling of communion with their fellows that the Algerians exhibited is an essential aspect of Meursault's character and one that gives him a dignity beyond the simple rules which society has incarnated in its laws.

The connection between *Le Mythe de Sisyphe* and *L'Etranger* is unmistakable. Although the essay analyzes human experience of the world and attempts to show its true nature, and the novel selects from human experience and tries to give it an ideal nature, Meursault is in many respects the Greek Sisyphus in modern dress. If extended beyond the obvious details, the analogy could become ridiculous because of the contrast in purpose between the novel and the essay. In *L'Etranger* Camus is concerned to convey the absurd experience rather than to examine it rationally as he does in the essay; nevertheless, the fact remains that both the god-like Sisyphus and the office-worker Meursault are aware of the absurd and through their awareness gain their revolt, their freedom, and their passion. Meursault's wish to be greeted by cries of execration at the end of the novel are no more than an expression of his total recognition of the absurd and all its consequences as they are developed through the complicated reasoning of *Le Mythe de Sisyphe*.

In the dialogue between the mind and experience that Camus presents to his readers, each work contains many ideas and attitudes previously developed, but it also introduces new concepts which sharply differentiate it from the earlier writings. The aspect of absurdity that denies an essential lack of coherent significance to the world is familiar to readers of *L'Envers et l'endroit* and *Noces*, and it is also experienced by Meursault; however, in *L'Etranger*—and again through Meursault—Camus introduces a broader concept of the absurd which is less optimistic and implies that the absurdity of the world is not merely passive but is a cruel and hostile force. Meursault is not presented as an ideal example of how to live in an absurd universe, but Camus does offer him as an example of a person who becomes clearly aware of such a universe, who suffers from it, struggles against it, and is finally defeated by it.

It is at the point of defeat that the question of Meursault's innocence arises. There is no doubt that he has committed a detestable act in his murder of the Arab, but Camus does not condemn him; in fact, the evidence is stacked in such a way that Meursault is condemned through a misunderstanding. It is not because he killed an Arab that he is executed but because he did not weep at his mother's

Abstract Man

funeral. If Meursault is innocent, then the implication is that society incarnates a malign absurdity. The force of this aspect of absurdity is emphasized by the story of the Czech which Meursault keeps reading over and over again in his prison cell; and although Meursault finds the story unbelievable from one point of view, it can be interpreted by the reader as a symbol of Meursault's destiny. Just like the son in the *fait divers*, Meursault is also a victim of a kind of intangible fate that has little to do with Camus' usual definition of the absurd. This particular aspect of absurdity is further examined and given dramatic form in *Caligula* and *Le Malentendu*.

It is also within these two dramas that the question of limits— hinted at in *L'Etranger*—is further clarified and investigated. In the characterization of Meursault, Camus implies that man cannot live happily or productively if all events are thought to be equivalent. To Camus, all actions are not equal, and a judgment of them can be made without invoking the aid of sources beyond human experience. It is this tenet of Camus' thought, implied here and analyzed in the dramas, that concludes the absurd experiment and evolves into the philosophy of revolt.

CHAPTER 4

The Theater of the Absurd

I Camus and the Theater

ONCE in a television interview when asked the reason for his interest in the theater, Camus simply replied that he was happy there. In the society of actors, writers, producers, and stagehands working together for a common goal, he discovered the warmth that was necessary for him to be able to combat isolation and to find happiness. As early as 1935, he was actively engaged in the cooperative Théâtre du Travail in his native Algiers, and it was from the experience in acting, writing, and directing gathered both from his activities with this group and the later organized Théâtre de l'Equipe that he developed many of his dramatic theories. Through the real dependence shared by the members of the acting company and by means of their mutual struggle toward a well-defined end, they created a community of solidarity in which the participation of each member was total; and it was within this community that Camus found the material servitude and the limitations which he felt that every man and every mind needs.

As might be anticipated, Camus uses the theater as a medium for serious statements about human life. Most outstanding writers of the twentieth century have attempted to reflect the current moral and philosophical problems in their works, and in this respect Camus' intent is similar to that of such French, Swiss and American playwrights as Anouilh, Sartre, Frisch, Dürrenmatt, or Tennessee Williams. However, Camus' resemblance to these men is only applicable in broad generalities. They all write plays that consider the doubts and aspirations of their times, that discuss serious themes, and that portray fundamental emotions; but the choice of themes and the manner in which they are developed varies with each individual author.

II *Theory of Tragedy*

As a playwright Camus has always thought mainly in terms of tragedy, for he felt that the audience's involvement was most intense in this form of the drama. He neither admired a theater such as that of a Bertolt Brecht, which constantly sought to criticize a moral or a social evil, nor was he satisfied with the drama developed by his brilliant French predecessors. He denounced the ornate, diffuse language of Giraudoux and the alien Catholic universe of Claudel. In his search for a more personally satisfying type of dramatic expression, he turned to the study of Greek and Renaissance history to ascertain the reason underlying the tremendous dramatic output in those periods. He found that during these stages in the development of Western thought, individualistic attitudes evolved within what had previously been a homogeneous society; and that as a result of the emergence of new ideas, the individual who propounded these concepts was placed in conflict with the group.

Camus reasoned that if tragedy is born from this conflict between two equally strong and equally right antagonistic forces, and if the Greek and Renaissance writers created the greatest known tragedy, then it would follow that if the present time possessed the same operative factors, it also would be capable of stimulating great tragedy. His concept of tragedy is essentially Greek, but it can be expressed in Nietzschean terminology. The two conflicting forces of man's passionate assertion of his freedom and his will to live are placed in juxtaposition to the irreducible natural order which dictates his mortality. These antagonistic forces are those at play within a drama such as *Oedipus Rex*. In the Sophoclean play the nearly perfect Oedipus must finally succumb to the will of the gods and admit his human limitations. Camus' experiments in twentieth-century tragedy—although he insists that modern tragedy should be independent and distinct from its predecessors—share this Greek tendency to portray metaphysical dilemmas rather than individualized and humanized emotions.

In his essay "Sur l'avenir de la tragédie," [1] Camus defines tragedy as the tension which results from the opposition of two powers in a forced immobility. One of these powers is the universe, which the Greeks personified in their gods, and the other power is man, personified in a hero like Prometheus who revolted against the divine order. It is essential to tragedy that each of these forces be equally legitimate. Prometheus must be justified in his revolt, but at the same time Zeus cannot be completely wrong. These two justifiable—

yet not totally just—forces must be kept in perfect balance in a tragedy.

Although there is no absolute right or wrong superimposed upon the contending forces in a tragedy, any given force can only be right up to a certain limit. The constant theme of tragedy, according to Camus, is the limit beyond which one must not go. The man who overlooks this limit out of blindness or passion and tries to enforce a power which only he possesses is headed for catastrophe. To be mistaken about this limit, to try to break the equilibrium of forces, is to destroy oneself. Along the limit, equally legitimate forces meet "dans un affrontement vibrant et ininterrompu" (1703). The outcome of tragedy must remain ambiguous, for to resolve the conflict would be to break the equilibrium and to interrupt the vibrant confrontation.

As has been mentioned before, Camus believed that the two great tragic epochs of ancient Greece and the Renaissance are notable in that during these ages, man's intellect questioned a preestablished sacred order and through this questioning created an atmosphere conducive to the creation of tragedy. This same intellectual attitude is prevalent today in man's revolt against his universe. Although twentieth-century man has neither the Olympian nor the Christian god to question, the Socrates and Descartes of today revolt against a universe of their own making. The world which man thought he could shape with science has become monstrous. Revolt against the cruelty of the old divine order has produced only more cruelty. History, which promised progress, has become as grim and implacable as destiny. Man, having set himself up as a god, now turns against this god. Thus, just as in Hellenic times and in the Renaissance, man stands before civilization in a state of rupture without having found something new which is satisfactory.

Contemporary man, who proclaims his revolt knowing that this revolt has its limits, who demands his liberty and submits to necessity, this contradictory man, distressed, from now on aware of the ambiguity of man and his history, this man is the tragic figure par excellence. (1707)

III   Le Malentendu

The first of his plays to be viewed by a Parisian audience was the Marcel Herrand production of *Le Malentendu* at the Mathurins in 1944.[2] Although the tragedy was his second drama—*Caligula* was written in 1938—it was Camus' first work to be conceived and written outside of North Africa, and it provides an excellent link with *L'Etranger*. The piece of newspaper that Meursault found in his cell while awaiting his trial contained an item that told of an unusual and ridiculous tragedy. A Czechoslovakian man had left his native village in order to go abroad and make his fortune. After twenty-five years, he and his family returned to the place of his birth. For the pleasure of a joke, he left his wife and child at an inn and without revealing his identity, decided to take a room at a hotel run by his mother and sister. Neither of them recognized him; and during the night they killed him, stole his money, and threw his body into the river. When his wife arrived at the hotel on the following morning and disclosed his name, the mother hanged herself and the sister committed suicide by jumping into a well. Meursault found the story unbelievable from one point of view but, from another, quite natural —"in any case . . . one must never fool around." Jan's desire to be recognized and to find his place in the world ends as tragically as Meursault's attempt to remain uninvolved in society and indifferent to the world, and it is Meursault's criticism of Jan's "fooling around" that forms the major distinction between the *fait divers* reported in *L'Etranger* and the three-act drama that Camus developed into *Le Malentendu*.

In *Le Malentendu*, man's strong drive toward love and happiness is in conflict with an absurd universe where everyone is irremediably lonely and all attempts at communication result in misunderstandings. By destroying the innocent men who visit their inn, Martha and her mother reflect on a human level the impersonal order of the universe, which is challenged by and brought into conflict with Maria's and Jan's desire for recognition and human happiness. Each of these forces has the double mask of good and evil. The two women are wrong to kill innocents, but their longing for an ideal world where "things are what they are" (II, 105),³ somehow justifies their acts; and although Jan's wish to bring his family happiness is noble, his coming into his own house as a stranger is a mistake. Since no limits are imposed on human action, no questions are asked, no depositions are made, and no verdicts are given, the play ends in disaster. Jan is dead, the mother commits suicide, Martha prepares to die in isolation, and Maria is alone and desperate. The only hope which Camus offers is the feeble one that if Jan had been sincere and could have found the right words, all might have been saved. Nevertheless, the conflict in *Le Malentendu* is resolved in favor of the universe. Human happiness becomes a matter of luck, and the solution to the absurdity of the world suggested in the praise of the physical life in *Noces, Le Mythe de Sisyphe,* and *L'Etranger* is shown to be impossible to those not born in a country of the sun.

The microcosm that Martha and her mother have created in their inn is an extremely pessimistic reflection of the cruelty of the universe, in which frustration of love and desire is inevitable and in the natural order of things. In *Le Malentendu,* Camus implies that nowhere on earth is man able to find comfort and feel at home. The room given to Jan is to sleep in and the world is made to die in. Destiny destroys the innocent just as the two women do, and even more cruelly; for at least they put their victims to sleep before throwing them into the river. Although Jan is murdered through a misunderstanding, the misunderstanding itself is not by chance. In a universe that has no place for hope or desire, there is an order. When Jan's wife Maria reveals to Martha the monstrous horror of her crime, Martha tells her, "So all of us are served now, as we should be, in the order of things" (III, 132).

This lack of recognition, communication, and understanding inherent in the world is strikingly underlined by the actions of the old servant. He speaks as little as possible, and then he says only as much as he has to. He has trouble hearing, and he misunderstands what is said to him. When, alone in his room, Jan seeks to escape the haunting loneliness and "the fear that there is no answer" (II, 209), he rings for the servant. The old man appears but says nothing. Again at the end of the play this servant comes onto the stage in answer to Maria's passionate cry to God for help. "Oh, God," she appeals, "I cannot live in this desert! It is on You that I must call and I shall find the words. . . . Have pity, turn toward me. Hear me and raise me from the dust, O Heavenly Father! Have pity on those who love each other and are parted" (III, 133). The servant answers "No." Whether or not the old man symbolizes God is debatable, but he does reveal the painful fact that man is alone in his suffering and that any appeal to a miraculous revelation from beyond the human realm is in vain.

IV Caligula

This same problem of suffering in a world which has no meaning is also central to the play *Caligula.* Camus uses Suetonius' story of the mad Emperor Caligula to develop and reject the notion that man can attain the ideal by adopting as a rule of life: "tout est

The Theater of the Absurd

permis." Like Martha and her mother, Caligula finds the world unsatisfactory, and in his attempt to refashion it by making himself equal to the gods, he, again like the two women in *Le Malentendu*, becomes a manifestation of the absurd on earth. The dramatic action begins with and is dominated by Caligula's discovery of the simple truth that "men die and they are not happy" (I, 8). Given the unsatisfactory state of the world as it is, Caligula tries to transcend death and misery by creating "a kingdom where the impossible is king" (I, 16). The death of his sister Drusilla has made him aware of the absurd and given him a need of "the moon, or happiness, or eternal life—something, in fact, that may sound crazy, but which isn't of this world" (I, 8). Other men have longed for the poetically impossible, but unlike them Caligula has absolute power as Emperor. He decides to use this power to create a kingdom of the impossible on earth. It is a question, he says, of making possible that which is not possible. When the moon is in his hands and the impossible is on earth, then he and the world will be transformed. Men will not die and they will be happy. His hope is that finally, "when all is leveled out, when the impossible has come to earth, and the moon is in my hands—then, perhaps, I shall be transfigured and the world renewed; then men will die no more and at last be happy" (I, 17).

In his personal attempt to transform the world, Caligula becomes a kind of apostle of the absurd. He ensures that all shall be forced to recognize, through him, the absurdity of the world. He decrees famine and execution, rewards a slave guilty of theft with the gift of a fortune because he has remained silent under torture, commands that the prize for civic virtue shall go to the citizen who has made the largest number of visits to the state brothels; in his every act he strives to equal the gods in cruelty, stupidity, and hatred. To demonstrate his likeness to the gods, he dresses as Venus and forces the people to pray to the goddess to teach them the truth of the world: that there is no truth. In spite of the obvious ridiculousness of his actions, the logic underlying them is never questioned. The audience is constantly made aware of the painful fact that the world is absurd, and that Caligula's actions—no matter how seemingly wrong—cannot be condemned. There is nothing in the nature of things that can prove him wrong. The world is absurd and he merely stresses this overwhelming truth.

Although the rules of logic cannot destroy Caligula, he dies knowing that he has failed. His statement that, "I have chosen a wrong path, a path that leads to nothing. My freedom isn't the right one" (IV, 73) invites us to find the reason for his failure in something other than the laws of logic. In pursuing his reign of absurdity, Caligula acted as if his freedom were limitless, as if all actions were equal. His rule is opposed on the one hand by the patricians who uphold the sanctified social institutions and condemn the idea of absurdity in the name of the gods or eternal values, but their opposition is proved ineffectual. On the other hand, the character Cherea, Caligula's confidant, resists Caligula's reign of terror for entirely different reasons. Without seeking to defend his position from any rational or religious viewpoint, he simply states that "some actions are . . . more praiseworthy than others" (III, 52). It is not a higher idea which makes him oppose Caligula, but rather a personally felt belief that all actions are not equal and that man's charge is to judge human actions and to set limits which cannot be transgressed. The world remains absurd, but Cherea introduces a concept here that will not permit uncontrolled freedom to destroy those needs which are basic to human existence.

Caligula's error was not his rebellion against absurdity but rather his failure to recognize the limits that are imposed upon human action. By destroying Caligula's kingdom of the impossible, Camus introduces a concept here that is more fully analyzed and developed in his subsequent writings. It is important to our understanding of his evolving thought to be aware that at this early date the concept of revolt and the idea of limits are adequately formulated, so that there occurs in Camus' philosophy a switch from an emphasis on the notion of absurdity to an investigation of man's permissible actions within an absurd universe. In a world without God and without any recourse to an absolute order, man is still not free to do whatever he pleases. There are limits, inherent within the nature of man and the world, that forbid those excessive actions which ignore the rights of others. Caligula finally recognizes this fact and admits his failure. He dies knowing that he is neither innocent nor justified. His hour of death, along with that of the characters of *Le Malentendu* and of Meursault from *L'Etranger,* is also his hour of truth. In the plays as well as in the novel, man is doomed, but through his suffering he becomes aware of a higher order of greatness which surpasses him. He realizes that even though this world has no hierarchy of metaphysical values, it does have bounds which govern and limit his selfish ambitions.

The Theater of the Absurd

V Relationship to Camus' Other Works

Like *L'Etranger*, *Caligula* and *Le Malentendu* are concerned with the moral distress in a human society that can no longer reach outside itself for a coherent system of ethical values; however, unlike *L'Etranger*, in both *Caligula* and *Le Malentendu* a stronger emphasis is placed on a spirit of revolt against the hostile aspects of the world's absurdity than on one against man-made standards of morality. Camus has refused to draw the nihilist conclusion that because the world is irrational, the irrational is the only logical principle of conduct. Discovering that the world is absurd, Martha and her mother and Caligula imagine that they can somehow transform it for the better. For the mother and daughter this idea is projected into their dream of the land "where summer crushes everything," and the means that they employ to attain their dream are never brought into question. Caligula inaugurates a capricious reign of terror and topsy-turvy morality in his attempt to transform the world by becoming the prophet of absolute absurdity. In his dreadful way he is awakening his subjects to the absurdity of existence, but this truth is an abstraction and Camus seems to be saying that men cannot live by abstractions alone. This idea is later more fully developed in *L'Homme révolté*, but for the moment the reader's attention is switched from the study of ideologies which corrupt man to nature which sobers him with reminders of his limits. Caligula is destroyed by a revolt, prompted by the instinctive recognition that his conduct has exceeded life's absurdity.

This is the rough draft of metaphysical revolt, rooted in the spirit of the average man who has braced himself against his fate and refused to take it lying down. In his 1955 preface to the American edition of *Le Mythe de Sisyphe*, Camus remarked that ". . . within the limits of nihilism, it is possible to proceed beyond nihilism." Despair, to Camus, has always been the ultimate sin, and he argues this point in his *Lettres à un ami allemand*. These letters to an imaginary German friend, originally published in the underground press in 1943 and 1944, introduce a concept of revolt strikingly different from the personal attitude expressed in *Noces* or *Le Mythe de Sisyphe*. In both of these earlier works, revolt was seen as an essentially sterile notion which aspired to nothing and was completely without hope. This is the type of revolt illustrated by the actions of Martha and Caligula in their attempt to fulfill a nostalgic longing for a reasonable world; however, in *Les Lettres à un ami allemand*,

Camus redefines the term in order to provide a means of escape from the private and solitary world of a Meursault or a Caligula into a world in which the individual is vitally concerned with man in society.

The most obvious reason for this change in concept is Camus' experience during the war. The events of the war vividly emphasized the interdependence of human beings, and Camus became increasingly aware of the relationship between individual happiness and the attitude and conduct of others. He saw that a world void of a belief in moral principles, in which the individual was free to act in accordance with his own desires, could lead to a total disregard for the life and welfare of others. In opposition to absolute individual freedom, he proposed an attitude of revolt that refused to add to the misery of mankind and that actively opposed those who did so. This new connotation of the meaning of revolt expressed in the four letters is further clarified in the 1945 essay "Remarque sur la révolte," but it is adequately formulated here to give us a clear insight into Camus' changing attitude at the time he was composing *La Peste*.

CHAPTER 5

An Invitation to Happiness

I *Publication and Reception of* La Peste

IF *L'Etranger* is the most frequently discussed of Camus' books, it is *La Peste* that is the best known. Published in 1947, it has been translated into sixteen foreign languages and has become one of the most widely read books to be written in France since World War II. The reasons for this popularity are manifold; however, the almost universal appeal of the book lies within Camus' strong expression of a compassion and respect for human beings that goes beyond any of the book's political, social, or metaphysical implications. Evolving from the earlier thoughts of *Le Mythe de Sisyphe* and *L'Etranger*, this central expression seems to mark a distinct change in Camus' philosophy; however, as is so often true in discussing Camus, what at first appears to be a rejection of earlier ideas is later seen as a development in or a reevaluation of his thinking concerning the fundamental problems of life. In *La Peste* there is no attempt on Camus' part to transform the world that he depicted earlier in *Le Mythe de Sisyphe* or *L'Etranger*, but the war years and the consequent human suffering of loneliness and death had sharply brought to his awareness the inadequacy of his earlier philosophy. In *La Peste* the emphasis is switched from the intellectual problems of the universe, the insignificance of abstract man, and the absurdity of his aspirations as they were presented in the earlier writings to the more personal problems of individual man and his need and love for the fragile joys of life. The world remains as absurd as it was in *Le Malentendu* and *Caligula*, but its appearance has changed. Man has discovered that he is no longer alone, and through knowledge of the fact that "the grocer and he are both oppressed" he can resist—if not transform—the world.

II *Plot*

On the narrative level, *La Peste* is simply a chronicle of the events that took place in the city of Oran between April 16, 194– and February of the following year. The book is divided into five major sections which are artistically handled in such a way that both the events and the style reveal the progress of the plague. The opening portion describes men's individual actions in a city as yet not officially touched by plague. The major characters are introduced and are seen doing business, arranging for journeys, and forming views as if everything and every action was still possible for them. The second part of the book begins with the statement that "From now on, it can be said that plague was the concern of all of us." Once the town gates are shut, the individual actions, emphasized in the first part of the book, give way to the more universal feelings of fear and separation shared by all. Although the description of Rambert's various attempts to escape from Oran make up a major portion of this section, the individual responses of the various characters are overshadowed by an analysis of the general reactions of the people. The individual is still seen in his heart-rending struggle to recover his lost happiness and to balk the plague, but by the beginning of Part Three he acknowledges the fact that there are no longer individual destinies: "only a collective destiny, made up of plague and the emotions shared by all" (151).[1] In this third section, no isolated actions are described. The individual revolt of the first weeks of the plague is supplanted by a vast despondency in which nothing is left "but a series of present moments" (165). Whereas in the early days of the plague the people of Oran had been struck by the host of small details that had meant so much to them personally and had made their lives unique, they now took an interest only in what interested everyone else; they had only general ideas, and even their tenderest affections now seemed abstract, items of the common stock. The deadening immobility described in Part Three lies in violent contrast to the vibrant descriptions of individual actions that make Part Four the most moving and significant section of the book. The poetic impact of the death of Othon's child, Paneloux's second sermon, and Tarrou's confession prepares the reader for the sudden and unexpected return of the rats to the city at the end of Part Four. The brief fifth section deals with the end of the plague, the reunion of lovers, and the complete return to the individual feelings and actions that made up the introductory section.

At the literal level, *La Peste* has very little plot. The narrative simply follows the plague from its beginnings to its eventual disappearance, and it can be successfully and absorbingly read as a chronicle. To do this, however, is to render Camus a vast injustice. The epigraph, which he chose from Daniel Defoe's preface to *Journal of the Plague Years*, states that: "It is as reasonable to represent one kind of imprisonment by another, as it is to represent anything that really exists by that which exists not." This quotation immediately invites the reader to transfer his attention from the literal to the figurative level of the novel and to see the intended richness and scope of the narrative.[2]

III   *The Dominant Theme*

For me, one of the most rewarding methods of attaining the meaning of this novel is realized through an analysis of the major characters and their relationship to the plague.[3] This approach is justified by means of a very simple and obvious interpretation of the all-encompassing symbol of plague. In the final section of the book, Dr. Rieux visits his old asthma patient. The distant clamor of the populace rejoicing in its new-won freedom from the plague can be faintly heard in the bedroom. Dr. Rieux and the patient exchange a few introductory remarks, and then the old man says, "All those folks are saying: 'It was plague. We've had the plague here' . . . But what does that mean—'plague'? Just life, no more than that" (277). Whether the novel be read as a symbolic treatment of the political problems of France at the time of the German occupation or of the metaphysical ones brought about by cosmic alienation in an absurd universe, the simple fact remains that Camus, in the words of one of his most interesting and bizarre characters, has equated plague with life. If the reader, in turn, accepts this meaning of plague, then the entire novel becomes a statement about life and death or—more generally speaking—about the human condition in the twentieth-century Western world. It is at this point that the reader's thought evolves from a specific concern with the action, time, and place of the limited world of Oran in 194– into a very real concern with the problems of life for all men in all times.

IV   *Character Analysis*

There is almost universal critical agreement that in general terms "the plague" as employed by Camus represents whatever threatens to prevent the fulfillment of human life within the given limits of an absurd world; yet such a general interpretation is personally unsatisfactory to the individual reader. He is left void of any positive approach to the factual problem he has long been aware of. He still has no pattern or formula to follow, no hero to emulate; however, if he turns from the eternal actions of the major characters to an analysis of the characters themselves, I believe the pattern can be found. These major characters—ever aware of the complexity of their life situations—are able to find meaning and happiness in an absurd world. It is especially the rather insignificant figure of Joseph Grand, the named hero of the book,[4] who embodies the central theme of the novel and can supply the reader with his sought-after pattern.

According to the chronicle, Dr. Rieux considers Grand something of a mystery man in his small way. Tall and thin, he seemed lost in his garments, which he always chose a size too large under the illusion that they would wear longer. Though he had most of the teeth in his lower jaw, all the upper ones were gone, with the result that when he smiled, raising his upper lip, his mouth looked like a small black hole let into his face. Also, he had the walk of a shy young priest, sliding along walls and slipping mouse-like into doorways, and he exuded a faint odor of smoke and basement rooms; in short, he had the attributes of insignificance. It took an effort to picture him otherwise than bent over a desk. Even before you knew what his employment was, you had a feeling that he had been brought into the world for the sole purpose of performing the discreet but needful duties of a temporary assistant municipal clerk on the salary of sixty-two francs, thirty centimes a day.

Ambition was not the spur that activated Joseph Grand; all he desired was the prospect of a life suitably ensured on the material side by honest work, enabling him to devote his leisure to his hobbies. His salary remained a mere pittance, but he did not draw attention to past promises. The department head had been dead for some time, and Grand no longer remembered the exact terms. The real trouble was that Grand could not find his words. Owing to Grand's inability to find the right words, he had gone on performing his obscure ill-paid duties for the past twenty-two years. According to him, he felt a particular aversion against talking about his rights— the word was one that caused him to pause. He also hesitated to mention the department head's promise, for this would have implied that he was claiming his due and would thus have bespoken an audacity incompatible with the humble post he filled. On the other hand, he refused to use expressions such as "your kindness," "gratitude," or even "solicit," which, to his thinking, were incompatible with his personal dignity. He was one of those rare people who have the courage of their good feelings.

He dearly loved his nephews and sister, his only surviving near relations. He visited them in France every other year. He had lost his parents when he was very young. He admitted that he had a special affection for the church bell in his town. Yet, to express such emotions cost him a terrible effort, and this difficulty in finding his words had come to be the bane of his life. He brought up the subject of his difficulty of expression each time he met Rieux. It suddenly flashed on the doctor what it was that Grand was trying to convey; he was evidently writing a book or something of the sort.

Grand finally unburdened himself to Rieux. For the first time since Rieux had known him, he became quite voluble. Though he still had trouble over his words, he succeeded nearly always in finding them. It was as if Grand had been thinking over for years what he now said to Rieux. Grand told Rieux of his love for and marriage to Jeanne. They went on loving for a bit and then they worked and worked so hard that they forgot to love. Owing largely to fatigue, Grand gradually lost grip of himself. He had less and less to say, and failed to keep alive his wife's feeling that she was loved. Years of poverty and the gradual loss of hope in the future ruined their love. One day Jeanne left him in the hope of making a new start. Grand too had suffered but was unable to make a new start. He could not stop thinking about her. He would have liked to write her a letter justifying himself. "But it's not easy," he told Rieux. "I've been thinking it over for years. While we loved each other we didn't need words to make ourselves understood. But people don't love forever. A time came when I should have found the words to keep her with me—only I couldn't" (75–76).

After Paneloux's sermon, something like a widespread panic began within the town. Rieux and Grand stopped for a drink. To the doctor's surprise, Grand asked for a small glass of straight liquor which he drank off at a gulp. Then, a moment later, he suggested they leave. Out on the street, Grand remarked that happily he had his work to divert his attention. Rieux questioned him about his progress. Grand explained what he really wanted: "What I really want, doctor, is this. On the day when the manuscript reaches the publisher, I want him to stand up—after he's read it through, of course—and say to his staff, 'Gentlemen, hats off!' " (94). Grand added that the manuscript had to be flawless. He invited Rieux in and read him the opening sentence: "One fine morning in the month of May an elegant young horsewoman might have been seen riding a handsome sorrel mare along the flowery avenues of the Bois de Boulogne" (96). According to Grand, the sentence he read was only a rough draft. Once he succeeded in rendering perfectly the picture in his mind's eye, once his words had the exact tempo of this ride—the horse trotting, one-two-three, one-two-three, the rest would come easily and, what was even more important, the illusion would be such that from the very first words it would be possible to say, "Hats off!"

The next we read of Grand is that he is acting as a sort of general secretary to the sanitary squads. We learn that Tarrou was included in the talks between Grand and Rieux. Grand unburdened himself with increasingly apparent pleasure to his two companions. They began to take interest in the laborious literary task. Absent-mindedness was noted in Grand's work at the municipality. He was constantly thinking of perfecting his sentence. One could see that the strain of overwork was telling on Grand. He was becoming subject to excessive sentimentality, and at such times would unburden himself to Rieux about Jeanne. The climax of his condition occurred at Christmas. From his car, Rieux caught sight of Grand with his tear-stained face glued to a shop window full of carved wooden toys. Rieux imagined a scene of long ago with Grand and Jeanne standing before a shop window dressed for Christmas, happy in the love they felt for each other. And Rieux thought: "a loveless world is a dead world, and always there comes an hour when one is weary of prisons, of one's work, and of devotion to duty, and all one craves for is a loved face, the warmth and wonder of a loving heart" (237). Rieux had to carry the old man to the car. In rapid succession four events occur: it is determined that Grand has the plague, Grand tells Rieux to burn his manuscripts, he laments his inadequacy with words, and he shows remarkable improvement the following morning. Grand's sudden recovery is highlighted by the reappearance of the rats.

The final reference to Grand relates that he had written to Jeanne and was feeling much happier. Also, he had made a fresh start with his phrase. "I've cut out all the adjectives," he said.

Briefly, that is the story of the hero of *La Peste*. Camus places none of the intellectual burden of man's condition upon Grand: Grand in no way mentally suffers from the metaphysical anguish of Tarrou or even the frustrating torment of Rieux. He is less concerned with abstractions than he is with living. Yet he too has his "seemingly absurd ideal" and rebels in his own way against the bureaucratic, routine existence he has been forced into. What Camus has done is to give us an average man, who, without knowing the philosophical language to express his innermost thoughts, is yet an exemplification of an almost subconscious awareness of man's accidental and transitory presence on earth. Grand acts "as if" he knows. He does all of the right things. When needed he is everpresent to do what he can to help alleviate the pain of his fellow citizens; he even sacrifices his most valued moments of work on his manuscript in order to devote more time and energy to the fight against the plague. He is consequently a superb illustration of Camus' statement in "Remarque sur la révolte" that the action of a trade union secretary who keeps his accounts up to date is "metaphysical revolt, just as much as the spectacular daring which sets Byron up against God!" True rebellion against injustice, according to Camus, lies in the humble task which helps man fight against it.

The actions of Grand also help to emphasize the inherent structure of the book. Throughout the first section, Grand's personality—his uniqueness—is gradually revealed, and he remains essentially an individual with his own cares and concerns. After the state of plague has been declared, Grand—as an individual—is less emphasized, and in the second part of the novel it is his involvement with the plague that is described. Grand's love for his wife specifically illustrates the fundamental theme of suffering and separation of all who love each other that forms a major portion of Part Two. The third division, devoted to general rather than individual actions, makes no mention of Grand. He appears again in the fourth section, and here his significance is underlined by his recovery from the plague. As might be anticipated, in this highly emotional portion of the novel, Grand is allowed the extreme luxury of sentimentality. The Christmas scene, before the shop window as he recalls the memories of his lost love, is one of the most moving of *La Peste*. In the final chapter of the narrative, it is Grand who is seen ready to begin again. After burning his sheets and sheets of manuscript, what he finds alive in his heart is his memory of Jeanne. He has written to her, has begun his laborious task again, and has returned to the individual he was—with the important difference that he now possesses a greater degree of humanity than ever before. Through the process of the plague, he unburdened himself and learned of his basic oneness with all men; now he is ready to make a fresh start, only this time he has "cut out all the adjectives." Even the uninitiated reader cannot fail to follow the progression of Camus' hero Grand, and it is through the depiction of Grand's very real and uncomplicated handling of the plague that Camus was able to combine philosophy and art and to make his thoughts readily available to a public not necessarily schooled in sophisticated existential thought.

It is Grand's actions that make more meaningful the metaphysical struggle of the other characters against the human wretchedness and pain caused by the plague. In simply doing his job well, Grand is faithful to the idea of serving men without aspiring to the eternal or absolute, and in this way he is very closely related to Dr. Rieux, the narrator of the action. Perhaps the least complicated figure in the book, Dr. Rieux fights the plague in the only way he knows. Trained as a physician, devoted to the task of fighting illness and death, he views the plague as an acute manifestation of his constant enemy, death. He allows for no heroic interpretation of his actions. In his conversations with Tarrou and Father Paneloux, he asserts again and again that his commitment is only toward man's physical comfort and not toward man's salvation. "Salvation's much too big a word for me," he tells Father Paneloux. "I don't aim so high. I'm concerned with man's health; and for me his health comes first" (197). Although he knows that any success he may achieve against the plague can only be provisional, he never regards this fact as a reason for abandoning the struggle against it. Rieux's revolt is man-centered without any appeal to the beyond. As he remarks to Tarrou, "Heroism and sanctity don't really appeal to me. . . . What interests me is being a man" (251). Rieux, unlike either Tarrou or Paneloux, comes to terms with the reality of man's condition and searches for no ideology which would allow him to escape this reality.

Rieux is in many ways Camus' spokesman. Like Camus, he violently protests against the unintelligibility of a universe which permits the infliction of needless suffering on human bodies and human feelings; and again like Camus, he feels an overwhelming compassion and respect for man and man's pursuit of meaning. Rieux's total empathy with the needs of man is neither blind nor sentimental. He refuses—and will refuse until the day he dies—"to love a scheme of things in which children are put to torture" (197). His attitude is almost an exact quotation of a remark made by Camus in a talk given to the Dominicans of Latour-Maubourg in 1948: "I share your horror of evil. But I do not share your optimism, and I continue to struggle against this universe in which children suffer and die."[5]

Camus' inability to accept orthodox religion, reflected here in the character of Rieux, is juxtaposed to the Christianity expounded by Father Paneloux. Paneloux's attitude toward the plague is completely different from that of Rieux. In his first of two sermons, Paneloux interprets the plague as being divine in origin and punitive in purpose. According to his technological principles, the human suffering brought about by the plague is willed by God and justified by the sins of the people of Oran. His militant form of Christianity demands that the true Christian accept the sacrifice and suffering of innocent men in the same way that he accepts the sacrifice of Christ. Both have been willed by God. The plague poses no new problems for the Father until six months after his first sermon when he, along with Rieux, witnesses the death of M. Othon's child. He admits his revulsion at the sight of the child's agony, but suggests that his feelings are caused by his human inability to understand the final meaning of suffering and that "perhaps we should love what we cannot understand" (196). Paneloux's demand that man should put aside his desire for rational explanations and accept God's will through faith is the subject of his second sermon. It differs from the earlier sermon in that he now refers to "we" rather than to the "you" of the first one. He no longer seeks a rational demonstration of the belief that good finally comes out of evil, but insists that this belief be accepted by faith. The only choice is to "believe everything or deny everything." He asks for a total acceptance of God's will and a complete self-surrender and disdain of the human personality, for only in this way can man make God's will his own.

Paneloux's position recalls that of Heidegger, Jaspers, Shestov, Kierkegaard, and Husserl which Camus had earlier rejected in *Le Mythe de Sisyphe*. Once faced with the absurdity of existence, none of these men has been true to it. All of them eventually destroy it by deifying the contradiction between human need and the unreasonable silence of the world and take the unjustifiable leap into an irrational explanation that resolves the antinomy between man and the world.

Paneloux and Tarrou share the desire to discover values which will enable them to combat an imposed evil of non-human origin. However, unlike either Rieux or Paneloux, Tarrou wishes to purge himself of all evil and transcend his human condition. His intensely personal aim to become "a saint without God," to attain a peace of mind with no feelings of guilt, is somewhat overshadowed by his more understandable desire to rid society of the plague. He identifies plague with the death penalty. In his confession to Rieux, Tarrou tells him of his childhood. The son of a public prosecutor, he was first exposed to the horror of the death penalty at the age of seventeen, when his father asked him to accompany him to court. Once in court, he found that his attention was exclusively devoted to the condemned man. He could no longer think of this living human being as merely an abstraction. The memory of the sandy-haired figure in the dock who looked like "a yellow owl scared blind by too much light" changed Tarrou's entire life. Unable to bear life at home any longer, he became an agitator. To his mind, the social order around him was based on the death sentence, and he felt that by fighting the established order he would be fighting against murder. However, in his struggle against society, one day he came upon a new form of plague. In witnessing an execution in Hungary, he experienced exactly the same dazed horror that he had as a young man in his father's courtroom. And he came to understand that he had had the plague through all those long years in which he had believed he was fighting it and that he had had "an indirect hand in the deaths of thousands of people." It was this experience which convinced him never to accept any argument that justified murder; never to have any consideration for "anything which, directly or indirectly, for good reasons or for bad, brings death to anyone or justifies others' putting him to death" (229). Tarrou realizes that he has not attained a state of complete innocence when he tells Rieux that "each of us has the plague within him," and that he knows that in this world, man's seemingly most insignificant action may be responsible for the death of another man. Yet he strives to achieve the state of the innocent murderer by willfully joining forces with the victims and not the pestilences of the world.

With Tarrou, plague takes on the specific meaning of the death penalty. It is an evil which ceaselessly afflicts all men, and which individual man can struggle against, learn from, and survive, but which he cannot totally defeat. Tarrou's longed-for condition of absolute innocence remains an unattainable ideal, but his emotional reaction against capital punishment puts forth the political protest contained in *La Peste* against a world where murder is legalized and human life is considered worthless. Tarrou shares Rieux's respect for individual life and in many ways underscores Grand's longing for understanding among men when he says, "I'd come to realize that all our troubles spring from our failure to use plain, clean-cut language" (230).

The desire for simplicity and directness which Tarrou expresses and Grand finally realizes is a facet of the book that is most openly linked with Madame Rieux, the doctor's mother. Because of her presence with her son throughout the plague and her close relationship with Tarrou, she is frequently mentioned in the chronicle; yet she actually neither says nor does much of anything. It is through her felt presence that she creates a tranquil, serene mood that is extremely difficult to describe. Tarrou stresses above all her "way of explaining things in the simplest possible words" (248). Her ability to act intuitively as if she knew everything without apparently taking thought relates her to other feminine characters in Camus' works. Like Marie in *L'Etranger*, it is Madame Rieux here who gives *La Peste* an essential warmth and restfulness that cannot be conveyed by any of the other characters. It is essential that woman's gentle love and intuitive understanding be expressed so that the longings of the male characters be better understood. As has been mentioned previously, the theme of separation is a basic one in *La Peste*, and its intensity is felt by each of the major characters. It is one of Camus' merits as an artist that this acutely personal feeling is specifically defined in only the most general terms. By limiting his description to an actually very vague mother-image, Camus has allowed the reader to project his own feelings onto the desires of Grand, Rieux, and Rambert for their loved ones.

It is Rambert who is willing to risk everything for the chance of personal happiness. During the period when the plague was gathering all its force to lay waste the people and the city of Oran, Rambert continued his monotonous struggle to recover his lost happiness and to prevent the plague from besting him. From his experience in the Spanish Civil War, he had learned that the only remedy against human anguish is found in the happiness that love brings, and he is determined to be reunited with the woman he loves. He tells Rieux that, "Man *is* an idea, and a precious small idea, once he turns his back on love" (149). Although he eventually gives up his attempts to escape from Oran and willingly devotes his energies to fighting the plague, his actions stem from his inner conviction that individual happiness cannot exist in a plague-infested world rather than from belief in any abstract ideologies. At the close of the book, Rambert is one of the happy few who welcome back their loved ones and for some time will be happy. He knows, "that if there is one thing one can always yearn for and sometimes attain, it is human love" (271).

In contrast to the happiness he allows Rambert, for Cottard Camus accumulates every form of violence except death by the plague. Cottard is described as a man "who had an ignorant, that is to say lonely heart," and he remains an ambiguous character throughout the book. He is a condemned man whose crime is never revealed. As the plague progresses and inflicts confinement on all the citizens of Oran, Cottard's anxiety is lessened; for the plague establishes a common bond between him and other men. In Oran all lives are threatened and no one is free to escape. It is the plague that allows Cottard a moment of reprieve and a loophole of hope, and he desperately clings to this hope until the gates of Oran are again opened. At the end of the book he is seen, divested of all expectation, completely anxiety-ridden, being led away by the police. Cottard—unlike all the other characters of the novel—had not learned the value of human existence. He is introduced to the reader at the time of his attempted suicide, and he never seems to progress beyond his moment of despair.

In *Le Mythe de Sisyphe*, Camus dramatically rejects suicide as an irrational evasion of the absurd. Human destiny, he says, with all its contradictions, must be accepted as it is and life must be lived in accordance with this acceptance.

Living an experience, a particular fate, is accepting it fully. Now, no one will live this fate, knowing it to be absurd, unless he does everything to keep before him that absurd brought to light by consciousness. Negating one of the terms of the opposition on which he lives amounts to escaping it. . . . Living is keeping the standard alive. Keeping it alive is, above all, contemplating it . . . the absurd dies only when we turn away from it. (53–54)

Camus here exalts the value of consciousness, which is one of the oldest parts of the humanist tradition, and it is quite fitting in a book like *La Peste*, which deals with humanist values, to have the negative aspect of the book presented by a character who, with "an ignorant, that is to say lonely heart," failed to keep the absurd alive and to find the fragile hopes and joys that he shared with all men.

V   *The Blend of Art and Thought*

I have devoted some time to the summary of the major characters of *La Peste*, for they carry both the central theme of the novel and also embody the metaphysical implications of the book. I do not wish to imply, however, that an analysis of the characters reveals the totality of the novel. To consider them apart from their setting is to ignore an essential dimension of the novel. As has been seen in the discussion of only the major characters—and there are fascinating minor ones—it is almost impossible to exhaust the significance of what the plague is made to stand for by giving it a single interpretation. Its meaning is carefully woven into all aspects of the novel, combining as it does the everyday elements with political and metaphysical ones in a powerful single image of plague. Camus makes the coming of the plague represent different aspects of human misfortune. The specific manifestation of this misfortune is illustrated by the actions of a particular character or of several characters, as the case may be. For example, there is no doubt that Grand's unhappiness is in part a result of the impersonal, mechanical aspects of much of modern life; or that all the characters, in one way or another, suffer the loneliness caused by the lack of communication among men. Yet it is the collective fate of all the inhabitants of Oran, suffering and dying from the epidemic, that fuses these themes and provides the novel with its focus. In "Remarque sur la révolte," Camus has said that, "In the absurd experience, suffering is individual. From the first movement of revolt, it is the adventure of all. . . . The malady which until then was suffered by one sole individual becomes collective plague." In *La Peste*, Camus expands the particular and temporal experiences of the people of Oran into a universal and timeless symbol of man's suffering. By showing a progression away from private solutions of personal problems to a collective reaction to a common problem, he creates a symbol of universal significance and · gives artistic form to his underlying philosophical thought.

Perhaps one of the most striking examples of this blend of art and thought is contained in Camus' description of the feverish atmosphere that permeated the opera company's presentation of Gluck's *Orpheus*. Here art becomes a mirror-image of life. One could even draw an analogy between this scene and the play-within-a-play scene in Shakespeare's *Hamlet*. For just as in *Hamlet*, in which the action on the stage parallels the action of the larger dramatic structure, here too the plight of Orpheus reflects the progression of action within *La Peste*. In Act I, Orpheus laments his lost Eurydice and the audience discreetly applauded. In the second act, only a few people noticed that Orpheus introduced some tremolos not in the score and that he voiced an almost exaggerated emotion when begging the Lord of the Underworld to be moved by his tears. It was not until the duet between Orpheus and Eurydice in the third act that a flutter of surprise ran through the house as Orpheus "staggered grotesquely to the footlights, his arms and legs splayed out under the antique robe." The audience rose and began to leave the auditorium slowly and silently at first, but "gradually their movements quickened . . . and finally the crowd stampeded towards the exits . . . pouring out into the street . . . with shrill cries of dismay" (180). Without extending the episode beyond permissible limits, this scene can be interpreted as a specific illustration of the horror that permeates Oran in general in the same way that the individual anguish of a Tarrou or a Paneloux illustrates the metaphysical torment of mankind in general. It should also be noted that the structure of the scene, from the audience's indifference through partial awareness to complete recognition of the action before it, parallels the overall structure of the novel.

The incident at the theater may be classified, along with the description of the Othon child's death, the episode with Grand at Christmas, and Tarrou's and Rieux's swim, among the most significant scenes of the novel. Not only are these passages emotional in content, but they are also emotional in expression. As if signaling to the reader the importance of the action described in these portions of the novel, Camus suddenly changes from the precise, almost detached, narration that characterizes the major portion of the chronicle to a highly poetical prose style that permits the reader to become briefly identified with the action. These poetic moments are infrequent, for an essential detachment from both the characters and their situation must be maintained in order that the reader can readily transfer his thoughts from the literal to the figurative level of the novel, and thereby be constantly aware of the symbolical inferences being made by the author.

There are almost endless examples of artistic techniques employed by Camus to convey the central meaning of *La Peste*, but perhaps enough has been said to convince the reader of the book's excellence. In the final analysis its effectiveness can only be judged by a direct reading. What we do unquestionably learn from reading *La Peste* is that as the plague bored its way into the lives of the people of Oran, oozed beneath locked doors and barred windows, crept into sterilized wards, affected rich, poor, happy, and wretched men, it did more than spread its horrible pestilence. As the plague became infectious, each person had to divorce himself from his individuality, unite his force with the force of others, and work for something beyond blasphemy and prayers that united him with mankind in general. The cessation of the plague could not be a final victory, for the plague bacillus is never cured but runs its course only to return again. After the pestilence subsided most people returned to their former selves, enclosed again the human wealth they had revealed for such a brief moment. But amidst the joyous celebration there were a few who learned to omit the adjectives, a few who were better men, who had learned that there are more things to admire in men than to despise. In the battle against the plague there was no victory, there was only the awareness that man, against all odds, can resist, if not transform, the absurdity of the world.

VI *Relationship of La* Peste *to Camus' Other Works*

As has been stated in the introductory paragraph of this chapter, *La Peste* represents a reevaluation or extension of Camus' thought, but it in no way negates the philosophy presented in his earlier writings. The world remains the same absurd world of *Le Mythe de Sisyphe* or *L'Etranger*, but here he investigates the possibility of finding a series of values not only to satisfy his own demands but also to be commended to others on universal grounds. "We need to know," he wrote in 1944, "if man, without the help of religion or of rationalist thought, can create his own values entirely by himself."

This need was acute for Camus, for at this time he was personally involved in a reevaluation of his own political engagement. Very briefly, Camus discovered, at the end of World War II, that the ideas he had editorially expressed in *Combat* during the time of the resistance were only tenable in a limited way.[6] The war situation had forced him to recognize that in an extreme situation one is justified in denying the value of human life by destroying it; but having reached this point in his thinking, after the end of the war he could not continue to sanction any course of political activity that threatened to destroy whole classes of people. He felt that the political creeds which survived the war were in many cases based upon ideologies that unjustifiably subordinated human life to abstract principles. In no way was Camus prepared to continue an editorial fight for ideas that contradicted his own conviction that a human life—regardless of the political creed of its possessor—is priceless in itself. He gave up the editorship of *Combat* in 1945 in order to complete *La Peste*, and as late as 1949 he refused to return and take control of the paper. This action does not so much reflect a change in Camus' original position as it does a disillusionment with the left-wing intellectuals of post-war France. That he was no less concerned with the political and social struggle than he was in 1938–39 or in 1944–45 is borne out by a study of his next writings, the plays *L'Etat de Siège* and *Les Justes*.

CHAPTER 6

The Theater of Revolt

I The Intellectual and Political Scene

UNTIL the end of 1947, Camus had dealt impartially with the opposing critical views of the East and the West. From 1948 on, however, he refused to conform to the ideas expounded by the intellectuals and neo-Marxists of the Parisian left-wing literati, and he openly identified himself with the democratic ideology of the West. It is at this time that the dichotomy between his literary and political activity, which had persisted throughout his earlier career, gives way to a desire to employ literature as a means of political influence. There is no doubt that when one studies *L'Etat de Siège, Les Justes,* and, specifically, the later *L'Homme révolté* that he is forced to deal with the French intellectual and political scene of the 1940's and 1950's. Camus' arguments with Mauriac, Sartre, and André Breton, along with his polemics against Communism, are vividly reflected in his artistic writing at this time and in turn clarify many of the underlying moral and political problems considered in the literary works.

For our purposes here, it should suffice to point out that after the war, Camus felt that the nihilism responsible for having brought the Nazis into power was now threatening the entire world. The actions of the United States and the Soviet Union demonstrated that the common threat of Hitlerism was not of sufficient duration to overcome the basic political mistrust and fundamental ideological differences that existed between the two nations; the United Nations was little more than an idealistic debating society; and, in general, world leaders seemed to have learned very little from the war. Because of the bleak international situation, Camus found it necessary to abandon many of the hopes he had held for the post-war world, but he continued to believe in the goals of world federation: freedom and justice. Although in October, 1948, he said, "I am aware that my role is to transform neither the world nor mankind," [1] he persisted in his battle for what he considered the most vital moral issues of the day. Because he was again suffering from the aftereffects of tuberculosis, he actively took but a small part in political events during the years 1948–51, but as *L'Etat de Siège*, *Les Justes*, and *L'Homme révolté* attest, he was constantly searching for the humanitarian spirit, lost during the nineteenth and twentieth centuries, which would again restore the value of an individual human life.

Produced by Jean-Louis Barrault, against a background of striking music by Honegger and an imaginative décor by Balthus—the former surrealist and friend of Joan Miró—*L'Etat de Siège* was first presented at the Théâtre Marigny on October 27, 1948. The cast was headed by outstanding artists: Barrault himself as Diego, Maria Casarès as Victoria, Pierre Bertin as the Plague, Madeleine Renaud as his secretary, and Pierre Brasseur as Nada. Yet in spite of the magnificent visual and aural effects of the production and the imaginative methods employed by Camus in his use of the chorus, of various dramatic styles, and of complex stage directions, in Camus' own words, "When *State of Siege* first opened in Paris, there was no dissenting voice among the critics. Truly, few plays have ever enjoyed such an unanimous slashing." [2] A work of art written by one of France's leading authors has rarely received such disastrous critical reception.

II *L'Etat de Siège*

The action of the play involves the conflict between the regimentation imposed upon man by abstract ideologies and the freedom of the individual, inspired by the natural elements. The plague, here represented as a human dictator, comes to the city of Cadiz in Spain. He is accompanied by his secretary, a woman who carries a notebook in which she has inscribed the names of the town's inhabitants. She can infect the citizens of Cadiz with the epidemic or she can kill them at once by striking their names off the list. The Plague usurps the political power of the city and institutes a reign of terror by inaugurating a series of laws which menace all normal human values and reflect all the worst features of a bureaucratic form of government. The Plague is assisted in his dictatorship by a drunken nihilist named Nada. A chorus of ordinary citizens hymns the beauties of nature which the Plague and his cohorts deny them. The chorus also reflects the changing mood of the people from confusion to anger to fear. Diego, a young man who attempts to alleviate the suffering of others, gradually emerges as the hero of the play. He is in love with Victoria, the daughter of a judge, whose love he renounces at the end of the play so that Cadiz may be freed from the domination of totalitarianism and nihilism.

The very fact that one of the central figures is named the Plague reminds the reader of Camus' earlier novel, and indeed the opening scene of *L'Etat de Siège* might very well recall the beginning section of the novel. Before the Plague appears as a person, there is a pantomime in which an actor dies on the stage; a doctor comes who first denies, and then admits, that the man died of the plague. However, once the Plague makes his appearance, the similarities between the novel and the drama rapidly disappear. In the *Avertissement* to the published version of the play, Camus informs the reader that although the subject is the same as that of *La Peste,* the play is by no means an adaptation of the novel. In the novel the plague was employed as a complex symbol of a force against which man can struggle and survive but which he can never defeat; in the play, however, the plague is specifically identified with a totalitarian force against which man can not only struggle and survive but also which he can defeat. The central problem of the play, unlike that of the novel, involves man's triumph over an evil brought on by a certain type of political government. The emphasis in the drama then switches from the general equation of the plague with all the forces of the universe hostile to man that characterized the novel, to the specific equation of the plague with a man-created, totalitarian ideology. Camus says:

I did not seek to flatter anyone in writing *The State of Siege.* I wanted to attack directly a type of political society which has been organized or is being organized, to the right or to the left, on a totalitarian basis. No spectator can in good faith doubt that this play takes sides with the individual, in that which is noble in the flesh, in short, with terrestrial love, against the abstractions and the terrors of the totalitarian state, whether this be Russian, German, or Spanish. (*Actuelles I,* 242)

It is Camus' avowed intention to create a modern myth which contains not only his analysis and criticism of twentieth-century society but also a possible solution to the problems he raises. At the close of the first of the three parts of the play, the Plague clarifies for the people of Cadiz the meaning of living in a state of siege:

So take good notice, sentiment is banned, and so are other imbecilities, such as the fuss you make about your precious happiness, the maudlin look on lovers' faces, your selfish habit of contemplating landscapes, and the crime of irony. Instead of these I give you organization. That will worry you a bit to start with, but very soon you'll realize that good organization is better than cheap emotion. (I, 171)[3]

In place of nonsensical ideas and righteous indignation, the Plague brings the people order, silence, and total justice; and it is against these meaningless abstractions that Diego eventually revolts. In place of the "wild roses in the hedges, the signs in the sky, the smiles of summer, the great voice of the sea, the moments when man rises in his wrath and scatters all before him" (II, 206), the Plague has sought to express everything in terms of figures and formulas, and to replace human values with a hypocritical and contradictory interpretation of justice.

The conflict between Diego and the Plague outlines in creative form what is to be later developed by Camus into his philosophy of revolt. Not only does Diego react against the abstract concepts of the Plague, but he is also placed in a situation where he must make a choice between submission and revolt. He cannot appeal to traditional standards or supernatural sanction, for these things mean nothing to him. Neither the church nor the law attempts to resist the plague, and Diego feels himself alone and frightened. Until he overcomes the fear and anguish within himself, he cannot act. It is not until his confrontation with death that he realizes that he is not alone and that many men are quite as much alone as he.

Each of us is alone because of the cowardice of the others. Yet though, like them, I am humiliated, trodden down, I'd have you know that you are nothing, and that this vast authority of yours, darkening the sky, is no more than a passing shadow cast upon the earth, a shadow that will vanish in a twinkling before a great storm wind of revolt. (II, 206)

Through the discovery that he is not alone in his universe and that other men share not only his fears but also his desires, Diego defines his own revolt in the name of the more fragile joys of life and is willing to accept all the consequences of his actions. He has thus acknowledged his total responsibility as a man; and completely independent of any metaphysical aid, he has fashioned his own destiny. In Camus' criticism of the empty absolutes offered by the Plague in place of the rich beauties offered by the world, as well as in his portrayal of a hero who, without any appeal to a supernatural authority, revolts against these absolutes, he has artistically asserted the position that man can triumph over the plague through revolt.

III   *Relationship of* Le Siège *to Camus' Other Works*

As if to underscore the threat that an empty society can inflict upon mankind, normal human values are shown to be threatened not only by the excesses of dictatorships, but also by the hypocrisy of bourgeois morality. In many ways, Diego's situation in *L'Etat de Siège* parallels that of Meursault in *L'Etranger*. Neither protagonist can find any satisfaction in the outworn dictates of the church or the empty rulings of the law. Here Camus continues an underlying theme of both *L'Etranger* and *La Peste*. Meursault's actions were contrasted with the banal and empty actions of the bourgeois world; and like Diego, he found no solace from either the church or the law. In *La Peste* the same theme is repeated in Camus' satirical protrayal of Judge Othon's family and Father Paneloux's failure to find an answer for man's suffering. These criticisms of dead and discredited values are again directly leveled in *L'Etat de Siège*. When the priest tells the people of Cadiz that the plague "is the penalty with which God has ever visited cities that have grown corrupt; thus it is He punishes them for their mortal sin" (I, 153), his words are almost an exact repetition of Paneloux's first sermon. And there is little doubt that Judge Cassade in *L'Etat de Siège* reflects the same hypocrisy of the law as that implied in *L'Etranger* and *La Peste*. He has judged all his life according to an idea of absolute justice that failed to consider "the right of lovers not to be parted, the right of the criminal to be forgiven, the right of every penitent to recover his good name" (II, 192). It is through the characters of the priest and the judge that Camus convinces his audience that the morality expounded by formal clerical and secular law contributes as much to the deadening atmosphere of the totalitarian state as does the autocratic power of the Plague himself.

Throughout the play, the empty, man-created world is contrasted to the natural splendors of the universe. This contrast again recalls a dominant stylistic device employed in all of Camus' poetic works. The world rich with "fresh fruit for the plucking, the poor man's cup of wine, a fire of vine twigs at which we can warm our hands" (III, 213) is ever present for man to enjoy, and it negates not only the monotony of the totalitarian state but also renders impotent Nada's nihilistic argument that, if only one could suppress everything and everyone, wouldn't it be fine! Lovers . . . there's nothing I loathe more. . . . And children, filthy little brats! And flowers that goggle at you like half-wits, and rivers that have only one idea. So let's annihilate everything. . . . Long live nothing, for it's the only thing that exists. (II, 178–79)

In *L'Etat de Siège,* Camus' rejection of nihilism repeats an earlier idea implicit in his letters to a German friend. Because there had been no other ideology to oppose Nazism, the Germans had discovered a reason for being, in the abstractions of totalitarianism. Camus seems to be saying that nihilism, with its denial of everything, has not only left man alone and adrift, but it has made him a willing receptor of any abstraction that will give some definition to his life.

As has been seen, *L'Etat de Siège* combines many of the ideas that we have come to associate with Camus' thought. He himself has said of the play that the "*State of Siege* . . . is, of all my writings, the one that most resembles me" (Preface, viii). Unfortunately, as true as the statement may be, the failure of the work as a drama cannot be ignored. Camus attempted to profit from the direct exchange of ideas between the playwright and his audience; however, it is exactly on the level of communication that the play fails most miserably. No one denies the beauty and nobility of the ideas expressed here, but the abstract handling of them produces indifference rather than involvement on the part of the audience. No matter how sympathetic we may be with Diego's trials, Diego himself is constantly dehumanized with words. Even the most anxiety-ridden of us finds it difficult to accept such verbosity as Diego's "O spirit of revolt, glory of the people, and vital protest against death, give these gagged men and women the power of your voice!" (III, 209). The audience is seen exhausted rather than stimulated by this inward-gazing dialogue that in rhetorical fashion constantly questions the "whys" of being. To believe in Camus' ideas, the audience must be able to accept the credibility of the actors who utter them, and this is impossible because of the unhappy combination of abstract ideas and highly stylized writing that characterizes *L'Etat de Siège.*

IV   Les Justes

Following the failure of *L'Etat de Siège,* it is amazing that within the year Camus produced what is generally considered to be his greatest dramatic achievement. Again preoccupied with the infinite power of revolt over a particular kind of political and social folly, he openly criticizes the Stalinist methods employed by the revolutionaries of 1950 and contrasts their actions to those of the just assassins who in 1905 refused to ignore moral limits in their pursuit of a classless society. *Les Justes* was first performed in Paris at the Théâtre Hébertot in December, 1950, with Serge Reggiani and Maria Casarès playing the roles of Kaliayev and Dora. In *Les Justes,* as in *Caligula,* Camus uses history as the basis for his plot. He borrows from the 1931 French translation of Savinkov's *Souvenirs d'un Terroriste* the factual account of the 1905 assassination of the Russian Grand Duke Serge, the Czar's uncle. Savinkov describes how Kaliayev, a member of the group of idealistic terrorists, at first failed in his attempted murder because the Grand Duke was accompanied by his niece and nephew, then later succeeded in throwing the bomb that killed the Duke, and finally was executed by the state in payment for his actions. Camus acknowledged his historical sources not only in the program notes on sale in the theater and in an article in the December 20, 1949 issue of *Combat,* but also in the Preface to the American edition of the play. He wrote that the "events recounted in *The Just Assassins* are historical, even the surprising interview between the Grand Duchess and her husband's murderer. One must therefore judge merely the extent to which I manage to give plausibility to what was true" (Preface, ix).

Inspired by the historical account of the revolutionary apostles of 1905, it is true that Camus borrowed heavily from Savinkov. Indeed, much of the dialogue of Kaliayev, Dora, and the Grand Duchess can be traced directly to this source; however, it would be grossly unfair to consider the play nothing more than a dramatic presentation of a historical record. Here the past is not recreated for itself but for the lesson it can give to the contemporary world. We are already aware of Camus' personal concern with the political atmosphere of Paris at this time and his dread of the hypocritical aspects of many of the current dogmatic pronouncements. *Les Justes* is in one respect an appeal to his contemporaries to reaffirm the integrity of the individual and to assume their responsibility in the pursuit of justice. In a letter, written to the magazine *Caliban,* he explains that,

The "modern" reasoning, as they say, consists in settling the problem: If you do not want to be executioners, you are choirboys, and vice versa. Kaliayev, Dora Brilliant, and their comrades, fifty years ago, refuted this base notion. Their message to us across the years is that, on the contrary, there is a dead justice and a living justice; and justice dies from the moment it becomes a comfort, when it ceases to be a burning reality, a demand upon oneself. (*Actuelles II,* 21–24)

The ultimate "demand upon oneself" that is made by Kaliayev is that he reject the momentary happiness and warmth of the world of men for the never-ending winter of the world of the just. This world is a lonely one, but it is the only one in which he can be a "doer of justice," and carry out his conviction that, "When we kill, we're killing so as to build up a world in which there will be no more killing. We consent to being criminals so that at last the innocent, and only they, will inherit the earth" (I, 245).[4]

The remarkable aspect of Kaliayev is that his motivation for murder is one of love rather than hate. Unlike the usual revolutionary, he bases his revolt upon a love for living rather than a belief in abstract principles. Before he leaves to assassinate the Duke, he confesses to Dora that hatred is not a sufficient reason for murder and that he must go beyond hatred to love, to "sacrificing everything without expecting anything in return" (III, 269).

Kaliayev's poetic idealism is contrasted to the harsh realism of Stepan. After Kaliayev had refused to throw the bomb because of the Duke's niece and nephew, Stepan expresses the thought of the hardened revolutionary who is willing to sacrifice everything to accomplish the aims of the revolution. In answer to Kaliayev's insistence that even in times of revolution there are limits imposed upon human actions, Stepan protests that,

There are no limits! . . . if you felt sure that, by dint of our struggles and sacrifices, some day . . . man will . . . look up toward the sky, a god in his own right . . . you would claim for yourselves the right to do anything and everything that might bring that great day nearer. (II, 258–59)

It is in these thoughts expressed by Kaliayev and Stepan that the essential difference between revolution and revolt is clearly defined. According to the revolutionary, his cause is just and must be fulfilled regardless of the consequences. He believes that all means which lead to the triumph of the cause are good. The rebel, on the other hand, is aware of limits imposed upon his actions, and cannot act outside these limits. Kaliayev refuses to sacrifice the lives and happiness of the men who are living today in return for the perfect happiness which the revolution might achieve in the future. The insoluble paradox then arises between the good and the evil which are parts of the same act. It is necessary for Kaliayev to kill the Grand Duke in protest against the misery of the Russian people. The ideal is noble and just; the act, however, is criminal. By killing another individual, Kaliayev has overstepped the limits imposed upon man by the natural order of things, and he has committed an unjust act in the name of justice. The only way that he can atone for his crime is through a willing consent to his own execution. He thus becomes his own judge and his own hangman. His death is his "supreme protest against a world of tears and blood" (IV, 291). Kaliayev's solution that the assassin must pay for his crime with his own life is the only solution that Camus accepts as valid, and in his portrayal of Kaliayev, he gives artistic expression to an idea that he further explains in *L'Homme révolté*: "He who kills is guilty only if he consents to go on living or if, to remain alive, he betrays his comrades. To die, on the other hand, cancels out both the guilt and the crime itself." [5] For Camus, the 1905 Russian anarchists, who constantly questioned their right to murder and who willingly paid for each assassination with their own lives, illustrate the limit which revolt can reach without betraying its initial ethical impulse.

In order to clarify the concepts of revolt and limits, Camus, again, as in most of the writings we have so far discussed, contrasts the richness of the individual's ethical and moral code with the hollow tenets of state and church law. In the third act of the play, the dramatic center switches from the relationship of Kaliayev with his fellow revolutionaries to the confrontation of Kaliayev with the forces of social order and justice. In prison, Kaliayev, like Meursault in *L'Etranger*, is questioned by representatives of orthodox law and religion. Skouratov, the chief of police, is not at all interested in Kaliayev's motives for his crime. What is essential for him is that Kaliayev admit his guilt and clear up the "slight untidiness" of the entire affair. According to his system of values, justice is only a matter of appearance; if Kaliayev atoned for his crime by informing the police about the other members of the organization, he would obtain the court's favor. Skouratov is deaf to any theoretical aspects of the murder. In answer to Kaliayev's statement that he threw a bomb against tyranny, Skouratov answers, "Perhaps. But it was a living human being whom it blew to bits" (IV, 282).

The Grand Duchess also emphasizes Serge the man rather than Serge the incarnation of an idea. Through her we see the Grand Duke as a man who two hours before he died slept in an armchair "with his feet propped up on another chair" (IV, 287); a man who through love shared his wife's sorrows; a man who spoke of justice in "exactly the same voice" (IV, 286) as Kaliayev. This man has been murdered by Kaliayev, and the Grand Duchess endeavors to convince him that it is his duty "to accept being a murderer" (IV, 288). According to the Grand Duchess, Kaliayev has only to acknowledge his crime for what it is and the road to God and salvation will be open for him. "God alone" can justify his act. Kaliayev, however, yearns not to meet God in a rendezvous on the steppes as in the St. Dmitri legend, but to come together with his fellow creatures on this earth. To capitulate and ask for grace would be to betray them and to isolate himself from them. His one strength is his sense of personal responsibility for his actions. By refusing to bargain either with law or with God, he regains his peace of mind and chooses "death so as to prevent murder from triumphing in the world" (II, 261).

With *Les Justes*, Camus approaches his notion of modern tragedy more closely than in any of his other three plays. In this play the particular type of tension which he insisted upon is easily demonstrable. Neither the Duke, as a representative of the existent order, nor Kaliayev, as a representative of the just assassins, is either completely right or completely wrong. Through the Grand Duchess we perceive an aspect of the Grand Duke that takes him out of the realm of abstraction and places him into the world of men. Although the ideology he supported was wrong, the Duchess' love and admiration for him gives him a new dimension and at the same time makes his murder a more detestable act than it was before. On the other hand, although the beauty and sincerity of Kaliayev's ideal is never questioned, he sacrifices a great deal of his humanity in order to obtain this ideal. He is the first to recognize that he overstepped the permissible limits when he chose to kill a human being for the sake of an ideal. Thus, neither rebel nor the object of his rebellion is either totally right or totally wrong, and the tension that results from the juxtaposition of these two forces creates a tragic mood of the highest order. This type of tension exists in all four of Camus' plays. Man is placed in a situation against which he must revolt. In the two early dramas, he rebels against the irrational nature of his fate; in *L'Etat de Siège* and *Les Justes* it is a specified tyranny and injustice that are the object of his revolt. Yet, in all the plays, in spite of the fact that our sympathies may center upon the rebellious, the forces that oppose him are also justifiable to a certain extent. At the moment of dramatic confrontation the fact that one force seems more just than another does not imply the inherent superiority of the one over the other. It is rather that at this particular chosen moment, the opposed force has gone beyond the acceptable limits.

V   *Relationship of* Les Justes *to* Camus' *Other Works*

Les Justes, like all four of Camus' dramas, reflects his philosophical concern with the doubts and aspirations of his own historical epoch. His plays are often difficult to understand within the context of his evolving metaphysical thought, but outside this context it is impossible to capture the full meaning of any one of them. I think that in part this difficulty lies not so much in the ideas presented as it does in the depiction of the characters who convey these ideas. One of Camus' greatest problems as a dramatist was to portray convincing people while exploring metaphysical problems. His dramatic world is not only a world without God; it is often a world without men. In the least successful of his plays, the major characters amount to little more than abstract expressions of an idea. No one contests the nobility of the ideas they express, but it is difficult for the average theatergoer to empathize with a character who with inhuman singleness of purpose gives himself totally to an idea. In his determination to combat the bourgeois complacency that he sees all around him, Camus lectures to his audience on the higher ideals of love of earth, love between man and woman, solidarity among men; and his lectures contain a directness of argument and a simplicity of plot that force the same audience to recognize the importance of these values. However, once the nobility is granted, the theatergoer is left with nothing to substitute for the stony happiness that he had before he was, so to speak, awakened from his lethargy. Despite the new force of revolt which he found for man, Camus never solved the problems of communication with the ordinary man; of the place of tenderness in a man's life; of how to find happiness.

In none of Camus' works does the absurd hero really establish contact with the crowd of ordinary men. The people are never mentioned in *Le Malentendu;* in *Caligula* the Roman populace is only reflected in the lazy, cowardly actions of the patricians; Diego saves the people of Cadiz but he never really communicates with them and he has to fight hard to refute the Plague's description of their cowardice and mediocrity; the revolutionaries in *Les Justes* love the Russian people but fear that this love will not be answered. Camus, the dramatist, faced much the same problem as that of his rebels.

He was aware of the difficulty imposed upon the playwright in his attempt to communicate lofty ideas to an audience composed of both imbeciles and intelligent people. Just as the clear consciousness of the rebel and the solutions found by him do little good if the gap between him and the ordinary man is so great that the latter is unable to profit from this consciousness and these solutions, so too Camus' dramatic skills and noble views have little impact if they fall upon deaf ears. The positive aspect of the willing sacrifice that the rebel makes in order to carry out his revolt remains extremely remote to the average man. The rebels' cause is unquestionably good, but the fact that their struggle for this cause makes neither them nor their world happier or better leaves the audience with a degree of doubt.

For all of Camus' rebels—Jan, Caligula, Diego, Kaliayev—revolt seems to preclude ordinary human happiness. They realize that the source of life is the love between a man and a woman and that to turn away from such love brings loneliness and isolation; yet they do not grant themselves the luxury of love. If their greater, or at least more noble, love for humanity ended positively, their sacrifice would be understandable; but their deaths may or may not help humanity. The only assurance the plays give us is that the rebels' deaths bring suffering to the person or persons who love them. None of the rebels in the four plays either finds or brings happiness. Jan leaves the sunny country and Maria and dies alone and unrecognized; there is no certainty that Caligula's death will add to anyone's happiness; Diego is satisfied with what he has done but not happy; Kaliayev feels a sense of victory but not happiness.

It is true that, given the state of the universe which Camus presents, if a man is to be faithful to his revolt he has no time to be young or happy. It seems possible though that this limited world is in part the artistic reflection of the state of things during and immediately after World War II. At this time Camus is optimistic about man but perhaps overly pessimistic about the universe and about the human condition. With some justification Sartre accused him of loving individual man but not mankind in general. The entire universe, past, present, and future, is not necessarily one in which man is killed for no reason, homeless, and a stranger. Camus did not live long enough to shake off the influence of the war in his dramatic work and to find a way for man to be happy. Besides, we have no way of knowing that he would have done so. Dora perhaps speaks for all of the rebels when she says, "We are not of this world, we are the just," and more than any other one thing, the insoluble conflict that is inherent in her cry separates the rebels from the rest of the world and makes us long for a world which contains much good if much evil, and many joys if many sorrows.

Camus, too, must have felt this need for a positive action that would bring a positive result. In his next major writing, *L'Homme révolté*, he endeavors to find moral values in a world that proclaims the death of God. In much the same way that Dostoevski proves through Christianity that values do exist, Camus sets out to prove that revolt in its true meaning is man's only recourse in a world void of religious faith. Following the ideas that are latent in the four dramas just discussed, Camus illustrates that revolt protests against the suffering and injustice of an absurd world and in itself creates a moral value based on the idea of moderation. He employs the solution to the problem of necessary political murder demonstrated by the just assassins of 1905, which is familiar to the reader of *Les Justes*, in order to illustrate the limits revolt must assert if it is to be faithful to its original moral impulse. Revolt now becomes specifically defined as the "impulse that drives an individual to the defense of a dignity common to all men."

CHAPTER 7

Man and Rebellion

I *The Philosophical Problems*

IN 1943, Camus argued in *Le Mythe de Sisyphe* that the certainty of death made life itself a charade and therefore absurd. He compared man's lot to that of the Greek mythical figure of Sisyphus, who was condemned by the gods to roll eternally a huge boulder up to the top of a hill, only to see it roll back down again. But from Sisyphus' seemingly futile and certainly never-ending task, Camus drew a particular kind of strength. Rather than surrender to a world without hope and meaning, he insisted that life and work must go on; indeed, it is from the very recognition and acknowledgment of the crushing truth of his absurd fate that man wins his own strange victory over the limits imposed upon him by his nature. Through his reflections on the absurd, Camus could say in 1943 that the only serious philosophical problem was the one of suicide; but confronted with the Hitler terror, the occupation, resistance, and final liberation of France, the Communist successes in France, and the events of the Cold War, he soon discovered that the stoic comfort offered by Sisyphus was of little solace or value. As early as 1943 and 1944, although still enmeshed in the theory of the absurd, Camus began, in his *Lettres à un ami allemand*, a search for some way to transcend the nihilism of his early writings; and in 1945, with the publication of the essay "Remarque sur la révolte," he moved closer to the idea of revolt as it is imaginatively presented in *La Peste* and logically argued and documented in *L'Homme révolté*. By 1951, the publication date of *L'Homme révolté*, Camus' thought had undergone notable changes. Because of the inadequacy of the absurdist ethic to satisfy the demands of his humanity, he undertook a reexamination of his earlier conclusions. Without negating the premise of *Le Mythe de Sisyphe*, he endeavored to find some satisfying answer to the absurdity, suffering, and injustice that man must endure.

II *The Purpose*

The general purpose of *L'Homme révolté* is stated in the introduction to the book. Just as *Le Mythe de Sisyphe* began with a meditation upon the problem of "judging whether or not life is or is not worth living"; so this work begins with a meditation upon the problem of "finding out whether innocence, the moment it becomes involved in action, can avoid committing murder" (4). To find an answer to the question he raises, Camus proposes to follow "into the realm of murder and revolt, a mode of thinking that began with suicide and the idea of the absurd" (5).

III *Reappraisal of the Absurd*

The idea of the absurd remains essentially the same as earlier presented in *Le Mythe de Sisyphe,* but in his reappraisal, Camus seeks to discover a mode of action that will teach us how to live in the world as it is. He does not dismiss the absurdist attitude, but he now sees the absurd as a limited perception among many possible perceptions. He sees it as a legitimate sensibility that took into account the universal malady of despair that existed between the wars, but one that does not provide values to judge human actions, to progress beyond nihilism, to create moral order. The reader, then, is first referred to a new analysis of the argumentation presented in *Le Mythe de Sisyphe.* According to Camus, the sense of the absurd, when one first undertakes to deduce a rule of action from it, makes murder seem a matter of indifference. If one believes in nothing and if nothing has value, it naturally follows that nothing is important and everything is permissible. Since nothing is true or false, good or bad, we should be willing to kill in order to gain the most powerful and most effective position for ourselves. As a matter of fact, the logic of this argument does not hold up under close analysis; for the absurdist doctrine, after having shown that killing is a matter of indifference, actually condemns killing in its most important deduction. Camus reminds the reader that the final conclusion of the absurdist process is the rejection of suicide and the insistence upon a persistent encounter between man and the universe. It is clear that through the rejection of suicide and the consequent recognition of human life as the single good, the absurdist analysis cannot logically defend murder. "Absurdist reasoning cannot defend the continued existence of its spokesman and, simultaneously, accept the sacrifice of others' lives" (7). Thus the same notion which permitted the absurdist to think that murder was a matter of indifference, now undermines its justification.

As soon as the absurd is interpreted to require one to continue living, it becomes contradictory in its content. The very act of living necessitates choice and judgment, but choice and judgment cannot be exercised in an absurd world. The absurd, then, considered as a rule of life is contradictory and unsatisfactory. It is not only incompatible with the act of living, but it is also incompatible with discussions of its own nature. Simply by being expressed, it gives a minimum of coherence to incoherence, and introduces consequence where, according to its own tenets, there is none. "The only coherent attitude based on non-signification would be silence—if silence, in its turn, were not significant" (8).

Faced with the insoluble contradiction raised by the absurdist reasoning, Camus discovers in this dilemma a new area for investigation. Although it is true that absurdism leads to a blind alley, it can by returning upon itself open a new field of investigation. The recognition of the absurd automatically implies the existence of some other value by which to judge it absurd. To have negated one value implies the acceptance of some other value. The absurd then is a movement of revolt that is affirmation as well as negation. And it is the affirmative aspect of the absurd that interests Camus at this time. In man's refusal to be what he is, in his insistence upon "order in the midst of chaos and unity in the very heart of the ephemeral" (10), Camus sees some hope for legitimate action that will end useless murder and allow man to act in accord with his individual human worth and potentiality. But before man can learn how to act —indeed, whether to act—the attitudes, pretensions, and conquests of rebellion must be investigated; and it is to this problem that the major portion of the book directs itself.

IV *The Three Consequences of Revolt*

In the first section of the essay proper, Camus seeks to define the terms "rebel" and "revolt." With a process of thought similar to the one he had employed in the past, Camus here uses an individual experience to clarify rather abstract terminology. In order to ascertain the significance of revolt, he begins by analyzing the relationship between a master and his slave at the precise moment when the slave decides that he cannot obey some new command issued by his master. And his refusal, according to Camus, has a double implication. The slave, of course, rejects the force which had oppressed him in the past; but perhaps more significantly, he insists upon his right not to be oppressed beyond a tolerable limit. Existentially it can be said that revolt represents the real moment of birth for the individual, for it is through his refusal to obey that the slave realizes his own value—independent and free. Up to this time he was acted upon, but through his revolt he demands respect for himself, identifies himself, and becomes a part of the community of free men. The first consequence of revolt then is to make the individual aware of his worth as a human being, of his potentiality as a member of the human race.

As the meaning of revolt becomes clarified, the slave arrives at a point where he refuses oppression for any reason and declares himself ready to die in defense of his rights as an individual. "What was at first the man's obstinate resistance now becomes the whole man, who is identified with and summed up in this resistance" (14–15). The slave proclaims the part of himself that he wishes to be respected as preferable to everything, even to life itself. Up to this time he had accepted orders and compromise; but from the moment of rebellion, a new awareness is born, an awareness of a universal good or value that all men—including the oppressor—possess. The slave becomes so convinced of his human right that he is ready to accept death and die as a consequence of his rebellion. And it is through this fact that he demonstrates his willingness to sacrifice himself for the sake of a common good which he considers more important than his own destiny. If he prefers the risk of death to the negation of the rights he defends, it is because he considers those rights more important than himself. Therefore he acts in the name of certain values which are still indeterminate but which he feels are common to himself and to all men. According to Camus, the analysis of rebellion has led "at least to the suspicion" that a human nature does exist. "It is for the sake of everyone in the world that the slave asserts himself when he comes to the conclusion that a command has infringed on something in him which does not belong to him alone, but which is common ground where all men . . . have a natural community" (16). It is the recognition of a universal human nature that is the second consequence of the slave's revolt.

The third consequence of revolt is closely linked to and follows quite naturally from the second. Camus concludes that the discovery of a universal human nature leads to the fact of human solidarity. When the slave revolts, he demands respect for himself but only insofar as he identifies with a natural community. His rebellion is always linked with his awareness of the solidarity of the individual with the human race, and he cannot act selfishly, for he alone is only a minute part of the values he wishes to defend. He needs to identify himself with other men and reveal that part of himself which is worth defending. "I revolt, therefore we are" is the formula Camus uses to summarize this concept.

In revolt, then, the slave—and ultimately all men— becomes conscious of what he is and what the world is, and he realizes his solidarity with the human race. He is still within an absurd universe, but he has learned that through revolt he can create his own values and proceed beyond the anguish of resignation and silence. Camus' intention is obviously moral in nature, for the type of revolt that he has in mind has little underlying self-interest and seeks to progress to a valid ethical ideal based upon the idea of moderation.

V *The Limit in Space and Time*

At this stage in the argument, Camus has defined and generalized the problem of revolt. He now proceeds to limit his discussion in both space and in time. For seemingly logical reasons, he confines his examination of the manifold manifestations of revolt to the Western world during the past two centuries. He justifies his choice first by stating that the spirit of rebellion finds little means of expression either in societies where inequalities are great or in those where there is absolute equality. According to Camus, "The spirit of rebellion can exist only in a society where a theoretical equality conceals great factual inequality" (20). It is our Western society with its seeming equality and actual inequality that provides the best stage for rebellion. His reason for limiting the major portion of his investigation to the time following the French Revolution is equally sound. Camus sees 1789 as the starting point of modern times, because the men of that period wished to overthrow the principle of divine right and to introduce to the historical scene the forces of negation and rebellion which had become the essence of intellectual discussion in the previous centuries. The murder of King Louis XVI symbolizes the secularization of our history and the dematerialization of the Christian God. Up to this time God played a part in history through the medium of the kings; but when His representative in history is killed, there is nothing but a semblance of God, relegated to the heaven of principles. With the death of God's representative on earth, man becomes free to attempt to discover a new illumination and a new happiness. It is from this historical moment forward that man is free to rebel, free from a society whose problems were resolved by an appeal to a God who created and was responsible for all things. Henceforth man must formulate his morality in reasonable terms, must search for rules of conduct outside the realm of religion and its absolute values.

VI   *Religion and Revolt*

Although orthodox religious concepts are eventually negated in Camus' search "to find a rule of conduct outside the realm of religion and its absolute values" (21), there is a strong underlying moral intention of revolt that emerges from his discussion of the relationship between religion and revolt. According to Camus, the rebel defies more than he denies. Originally he does not suppress God; he protests against the human condition both for its incompleteness because of death and its wastefulness because of evil; and in his rejection of his mortality, he refuses to recognize God or the power that compels him to live in this condition. The metaphysical rebel is therefore not so much an atheist as he is a blasphemer, for his protest can only have meaning if he first posits an omnipotent God; and his revolt does not become atheistic until he subjects God to human judgment and deprives Him of His power. In his demand for equality with God, the rebel usurps the power once granted to God and alone assumes the responsibility for the creation of justice, order, and unity that he formerly sought in vain. He then begins to mold the dominion of man. If he remains faithful to his original purpose and does not abandon himself to complete negation or total submission, his revolt will be positive. It is his failure to remain true to the positive aspects of his revolt that eventually leads him to betray the moral value implicit in his revolt and to chose the comfort of tyranny or slavery.

VII   *History of Revolt*

At this point in the essay, Camus begins to describe the history of revolt in the Western world. It would perhaps be more accurate to say that he discusses the perversions of revolt. First, there is the metaphysical nihilism that demands of God absolute freedom for the individual and defeats itself in a mystifying dandyism; second, the abstract declaration of democratic values that produced the revolutionary tyranny of 1793; third, the Hegelianism that identifies rebellion with history and enslaves man in dialectic; fourth, the irrational terrorism of fascism; and finally the rational terrorism of Stalinism. Thus Camus pursues the history of a tradition of rebellion ultimately destroyed by a dehumanizing revolution. In the final section of the essay, disillusioned by the long, murderous, and deceptive history, Camus returns to the humanistic ideals of the Renaissance and rediscovers justness and proportion in the Mediterranean culture of Spain, Italy, Greece, and North Africa. Thus the total movement of the essay proceeds to the final exposure of the paradox whereby revolt in the name of freedom and justice flounders and collapses if it is not directed toward a system of ethics which could serve a world beyond nihilism.

VIII *Metaphysical Rebellion*

It would be tedious and unnecessarily involved to paraphrase Camus' comments on the history of revolt from Sade onward; however, it is necessary to elucidate some of his major thoughts in order to follow the movement of his discussion. In the section of the book devoted to metaphysical rebellion, he argues that during the past one hundred and fifty years, the same human protest has been repeated over and over again. From Sade onward, all metaphysical rebels, regardless of their different guises, affirmed the solitude of man and the absence of any kind of morality. But once having denied the existence of God, they then set about to reconstruct creation according to their own concepts and consequently to usurp the power that traditionally was God's. Although Sade's and the Romantics' original intent was in accord with the nature of rebellion, the rebels of the past have ultimately been unfaithful to the true nature of revolt. According to Camus, the rebel must seek a moral philosophy or religion that demands unity in the world, even if the world denies that life has any meaning. As soon as the rebel lays aside this demand and abandons the tension that it implies, for the world of appearances or for murder and destruction, he has rejected the burden of rebellion and destroyed the noble end that he initially sought.

IX *Dostoevski and Nietzsche*

It is the logical revolt of Dostoevski and Nietzsche that is the most appealing to Camus. These two men, above all others, denied God in the hope of achieving a more profound existence for man. Unlike the Romantics who sought to raise themselves to the level of God, Dostoevski places God on trial, ultimately rejects Him, and attempts to replace the reign of grace with the reign of justice. He does not endeavor to reform anything in creation, but rather he sets out to claim the right to free himself from all moral bonds and to reject all law other than his own. Nietzsche proceeds a step further. He rids the world of God and of moral values, and leaves man alone and without a master. The logic of Dostoevski's character Ivan Karamazov, "if nothing is true, everything is permitted" is replaced by the profounder statement by Nietzsche, "if nothing is true, nothing is permitted." Nietzsche thus avoids Ivan Karamazov's ethical dilemma, but he in turn subjects man to the heartbreaking task of accepting everything. Both Dostoevski and Nietzsche sought a reign of justice for man in logical rather than moral revolt, but their unwillingness to go beyond nihilism doomed their revolts to passive acceptance of the world as it is and to ultimate failure. Since both Dostoevski and Nietzsche affirm the sovereignty of the individual, no one man's actions can be judged as criminal or sinful. Man is again alone and his revolt has led only to a desert of solitude in which the solidarity of all men can never exist.

Camus views the revolt of the nineteenth century as primarily individualistic in nature and negative in its results. Since it failed to escape from nihilism, it inevitably led to a kind of anarchy which was easily perverted to justify detrimental action. Thus the revolt of Dostoevski led to the justification of revolution just as surely as Nietzsche's ideas became the foundation of Nazism. The fact that Dostoevski's and Nietzsche's ideas were misunderstood by the revolutionaries and the National Socialists in no way lessens the lethal effect that these ideas perpetuated. In their demand for what Camus calls the intemperance of absolutism—their desire for the absolute in philosophy—these men betrayed the initial concept of revolt and relegated the integrity of the individual to second place. In the teachings of true revolt, no man can demand for himself more liberty than is consistent with the liberty of his neighbor. Rebels such as Lautréamont and Rimbaud were equally guilty of absolutism. Initially, these poets purely expressed the idea of revolt, but as soon as they wearied of the effort demanded by their revolt, they almost automatically ended in banal conformism. The early poetry of Lautréamont and Rimbaud lies in direct contrast to their later work or life. *Les Chants de Maldoror* and Rimbaud's poetry are pure expressions of revolt, but *Les Poésies* and Rimbaud's later life clearly indicate both poets' failure to sustain the effort demanded by absolute revolt. The ideas expressed in *Les Poésies* and Rimbaud's letters from Harrar illustrate the poets' absolute conformity to banality.

X *Twentieth-Century Rebellion*

In the twentieth century, the individualistic revolt of the nine-teenth century degenerates into a combination of subjective anarchy and the objective principles of Marxism. The surrealists whom Camus cites as his witnesses are as guilty as Lautréamont and Rimbaud of stifling their revolt in dismal conformity. Absolute rebellion, total insubordination, and the humor and cult of the absurd were the terms the surrealists employed to define their primary intent; but unable to reach the goals of their movement, they sought to reconcile their subjective aims with Marxism. Because of two basic contradictions in principles, the combination had to fail. In the first place, in its insistence upon the submission of the irrational, Marxist theory directly opposed the surrealists' defense of irrationality; and secondly, while Marxism tended toward the conquest of totality, surrealism tended toward unity. The surrealists sought to reconcile Marx's "let us transform the world" with Rimbaud's "let us change life"; but since the first leads to the conquest of the totality of the world and the second to the unity of life, the desired reconciliation remained an impossible dream.

According to Camus, neither the individualistic rebellion of the nineteenth century nor the subjective anarchy of the twentieth century has retained the tension necessary to true rebellion. He sees the blind acceptance of what exists just as destructive to rebellion as the total rejection of what exists. In either case, the intended rebellion assumed only one of the terms of the perpetual tension which must exist if rebellion is not to be faithless to itself. While the tension remained, moral value could exist; but once the tension was eliminated, only death, violence, and moral nihilism remained. The only true rebellion open to man must retain its moral intention; for from the moment man decides to exclude himself from grace and to live by his own means, the only kingdom open to him is the kingdom of justice. This kingdom, for Camus, cannot be won by political conquest; for if metaphysical rebellion joins forces with revolutionary movements, the rebel abandons his original desire for the conquest of his own existence and sets out in search of world conquest by way of an infinitely multiplied series of murders.

XI *Revolt in History*

It is to the investigation of revolt in history that Camus now turns his attention. Just as the history of metaphysical rebellion began with Sade, he sees the time of historical rebellion as beginning with

Sade's contemporaries, the regicides, "who attack the incarnation of divinity without yet daring to destroy the principle of eternity" (108). However, before beginning his discussion of the history of revolution, he draws a careful distinction between his understanding of the word "rebellion" and "revolution." Rebellion, to him, is no more than an incoherent pronouncement that leads into the realm of ideas, whereas revolution originates in the realm of ideas and seeks to inject these ideas into historical experience. In his words, "While even the collective history of a movement of rebellion is always that of a fruitless struggle with facts, of an obscure protest which involves neither methods nor reason, a revolution is an attempt to shape action into ideas, to fit the world into a theoretic frame" (106). Although it may be initiated by revolt, revolution, because of its effort to establish a new social order at the expense of the existing order, inevitably introduces the idea that expediency is a sufficient justification for any and all action. Once murder, conquest, and enslavement are legitimatized, the original cause of revolt "to affirm the dignity of man in defiance of things that deny its existence" (105) gives way to ideological absolutism, and the rights of each individual to a measure of human happiness have been sacrificed to a vague promise of some far-distant perfect social order.

Camus dates the beginning of modern times in the year 1789, because the men of that period wished to overthrow the principle of the divine right of kings and to introduce the forces of negation and rebellion to the historical scene. Justifying their actions with Rousseauistic theories, these men sought to affirm the divinity of the people to the degree that the will of the people coincided with the will of nature and of reason. Reason, then, became the new deity for them and replaced the traditional concept of God. Although God was not yet "dead," a new religion that worshipped reason and virtue came into being. From 1789 onward the reign of the king was superseded by the reign of "holy humanity," and just as God was replaced by reason and virtue, so also was the king executed and replaced by the general will of the people. The regicides of 1792, through their execution of Louis XVI, succeeded in ridding their world of the last representative of God's law on earth, but God still existed as an abstract principle. It was not until the advent of Hegelianism that even this concept of God was denied and the reign of history began. Man, identifying himself only with history, from that time forward denies all forms of morality and desperately attempts to achieve the unity of the human race by means of a ruinous series of crimes and wars. The Jacobin Revolution, which failed in its attempts to institute the religion of virtue, is now followed by the cynical revolutions which try to found the religion of man.

XII *Hegel*

It is with the German philosopher Hegel, then, that the idea of God is finally destroyed. The principles of justice, reason, and truth which were consecrated by the French Revolution are now relegated to the end of history and can be attained only when the process we call history ends. According to Hegel, there are no values other than those sanctioned by the historical process. The reasonable absolutes that were recognized by Rousseau and Saint-Just as guides for action, now become goals in themselves that must be conquered by action. To Camus, the historical Absolute that Hegel postulates in place of God is a further dehumanization of the idea of revolution; for if man has no control over his own destiny and is only a part of the inevitable historical process, his individual actions cannot definitively be judged as either right or wrong. Further, if history is the only judge of action, it necessarily follows that the conqueror is always right and the defeated is always wrong, because it is only the conqueror who can move on with the flow of history. Moral values as such must then constantly shift and be adapted to the historical times. If an individual seeks to express values other than those sanctioned by the historical moment, his murder can always be justified in the name of some eventual good. Under this system the rights of the individual must be sacrificed to the state, and those who hinder the realization of the state must be killed.

It is not surprising that Camus concludes that all forms of totalitarianism derive their justification from Hegel. According to his reasoning in *L'Homme révolté*, radical Hegelianism has perfected the philosophy of efficacity and has transformed the history of revolt by calling man into action to bring about the final realization of his human nature. This placement of the fulfillment of real human nature at the end of the historical process is in complete disagreement with the philosophy of revolt. It will be remembered that one of the first consequences of the slave's rebellion was his recognition of his solidarity with the human race. If, as in Hegelianism, the recognition is postponed to an indefinite future time, then man becomes a slave of the future and is eventually ignored, repressed, disciplined, and even murdered for the greater good of the state. In the historical process, the present is only important as a step to the future, and man is used as a means to an end. This idea is in direct opposition to Camus' constant insistence in all of his major writings that man must be regarded as an end in himself. According to Camus, the consequences of radical Hegelian thought are eventually seen in the rational and irrational state terrorism of the twentieth century, but for the moment he pauses in the midst of his discussion of the general movement of revolutionary thought to recount the story of the *meurtriers délicats* as the unique example of fidelity to the values of revolt.

XIII   Les meurtriers délicats

Camus insists that the 1905 Russian terrorists, whom he calls the *meurtriers délicats*, marked the highest peak of revolutionary momentum. This small group of young men and women aimed through their assassination of the Grand Duke Serge to recreate a community founded on love and justice. In this respect they were no different from the hundreds of other dedicated men and women who preceded them in time and who also sought to create new values through attempted assassinations. What distinguishes this particular group from all others is that they, tortured by contradictions, gave birth to a value which from that time forward opposed tyranny and helped authentic liberation. In their ability to combine in themselves a respect for human life in general and a contempt for their own lives, and in their recognition of the inevitability of violence and their own inability to justify it, they lived the tensions and the paradoxes that Camus finds so necessary to revolt. Because they were able to keep the terms of both the paradoxes alive and were willing to pay for their guilt with their own lives, they were able to preserve the true character of revolt in a way that later revolutions were unable to sustain. As we have seen in the discussion of Camus' drama *Les Justes*, the 1905 Russian anarchists, who constantly questioned their right to murder and who willingly paid for each assassination with their own lives, illustrate the limit which revolt can reach without betraying its initial ethical impulse.

This triumph of the 1905 terrorists over nihilism was, however, extremely short-lived. Their individual terrorism that so successfully proclaimed the inherent dignity of man soon gave way to the well-known horrors of the state terrorism of this century. In the Nazi and Fascist regimes that claimed to be based upon the philosophies of Nietzsche and Hegel, the rights of individual man were usurped, and the historical situation rather than man became the arbiter of moral values. In both Hitler's and Mussolini's attempts to construct empires based on state terrorism and irrational terror, the dictators chose to deify the irrational, and the irrational alone, instead of deifying reason. They were the first to construct a state on the concept that "everything is meaningless and that history is only written in terms of the hazards of force" (178). The historical fact that their hopes to dominate the world failed is according to Camus implicit in the underlying tenets of their philosophies. They never really had any pretensions to a universal empire, even though they aimed at the eventual domination of the world. "At the very most, Hitler . . . was diverted from the provincial origins of his movement toward the indefinite dream of an empire of the Germans that had nothing to do with the universal City" (186). On the contrary, the dream of world-unification is to Camus the aspiration of Russian Communism and not that of Fascism. "Russian Communism . . . has appropriated the metaphysical ambition that this book describes, the erection, after the death of God, of a city of man finally deified" (186).

XIV *Karl Marx*

In the next section of *L'Homme révolté*, Camus exerts considerable effort to clarify the ideological basis of Russian Communism. In the English translation of his work, almost sixty pages are devoted to the criticism of the state terrorism that resulted from the teachings of Karl Marx. This fact alone accounts for the tremendous success the book enjoyed among right-wing intellectuals in both France and abroad; but as was true in his criticism of Nietzsche and Hegel, here too Camus distinguishes between Marxist theories and the interpretation or manifestation of these theories in fact. He points out that the Marxists who have made history have extracted the prophetic and apocalyptic aspects of Marx's doctrine without remaining faithful to the method he outlined in his writings. However, again as in the case of Nietzsche and Hegel, Camus sees inherent contradictions and inconsistencies in Marx's basic doctrine; and it is to the discussion of these contradictions that he devotes most of his energies.

Although Marx claims that his theories are based on pure reason, Camus finds them to be no more founded on reason than any other prophetic faith. He sees Marx's method as a mixture of determinism and prophecy that has a great deal in common with Christianity and the bourgeois culture. Like Christianity, Marxism superimposes

Man and Rebellion

an ideological structure on the world that it rejects and then awaits the apocalypse; and like the bourgeois culture, it reflects an optimistic belief in the technical and scientific progress that will eventually aid man in his attempt to conquer nature. Unlike Christianity, Marxism replaces God and all transcendent principles with a belief in a future Utopia; and in its relegation of values to the future, it loses its scientific foundation and becomes no more or no less than any other supposition.

Camus also sees a contradiction within Marx's untenable belief in the dialectical concept of history. He argues that complete acceptance of the dialectical principle negates the end of history to which the Marxist revolution directs itself. Since the Marxist dialectic is only pure movement which seeks to negate all that is other than itself, it cannot imply an end to something that by admission has no beginning. The very nature then of the dialectic refutes Marx's belief that the class struggle would eventually be replaced by a classless society; for by necessity, once the classless society was attained, a new undefined antagonism would have to come into being.

These discrepancies in Marx's theory, coupled with his failure to foresee the development of society as it actually occurred, led to an eventual reinterpretation and bastardization of his system by the Russian Communists. What Camus deplores the most in contemporary Marxism is its failure to remain faithful to the original spirit of revolt. Ignoring its initial insistence upon the innocence of man, revolt, in the hands of the Russian Communists, denies the existence of a human nature and ignores every moral precept. Methods of thought which originally claimed an intent to realize the total man have disintegrated into an acceptance of the logic of history and the mutilation and destruction of men.

To the slave's, "I rebel, therefore we exist," metaphysical rebellion had added, "We are alone," and attempted to construct existence with appearances. Now, absolute revolution has carried the original statement even further by supposing the malleability of human nature and its possible reduction to the conditions of a historical force. According to Camus, revolution has betrayed rebellion in two ways. First, in its attempt to establish a perfect social order, the world of power is constantly at odds with the less than perfect human nature that rebellion affirms. Secondly, revolution, in its rush to attain its longed for social order, justifies the murder of those men who detain its progress, and in this way it surpasses the limits that rebellion sets for itself. Furthermore, through its affirmation of "a limit, a dignity, and a beauty common to all men," rebellion advanced toward a unity that is denied by historical revolution's demand for totality.

The former starts from a negative supported by an affirmative, the latter from absolute negation and is condemned to every aspect of slavery in order to fabricate an affirmative that is dismissed until the end of time. . . . The first is dedicated to creation so as to exist more and more completely; the second is forced to produce results in order to negate more and more completely. (251)

Rebellion says that revolution must try to act, not in order to come into existence at some future date, but in terms of the obscure existence that is already made manifest in the act of insurrection. To the "I rebel, therefore we exist" and the "We are alone" of metaphysical rebellion, rebellion at grips with history adds that, "instead of killing and dying in order to produce the being that we are not, we have to live and let live in order to create what we are" (252). Since this rule is neither formal nor subject to history, Camus feels that it can best be described by examining it in its pure state of artistic creation.

XV *Artistic Creation and Revolt*

In the next section of *L'Homme révolté*, Camus discusses the relationship between artistic creation and revolt. He correlates man's desire for unity and beauty expressed in art with his desire for order expressed in political institutions, and he affirms the ability of art to correct material disorder and to give man his longed for refuge from the all-consuming movement of time. The major points of Camus' esthetic theories, taken up in this section of *L'Homme révolté*, will be discussed in Chapter 9 of this book; however, it should be pointed out here that this particular section serves as an excellent bridge between the logical accounting of the history of revolt and the poetic presentation of the kind of revolt recommended in the final chapter of the essay.

XVI *The Dilemma*

After the involved investigations of error, treason, and darkness that constitute the major sections of the essay, it appears that rebellion is caught in an irreconcilable dilemma. Although the rebel has a clear concept of justice, as soon as he acts, he finds himself committing injustice. We have seen in the course of the essay that after metaphysical revolt destroyed the concept of God, the revolutionary expression of revolt ended in the murder of men. But murder cannot be reconciled with revolt. By definition revolt affirms the liberty of all men in face of a common destiny, whereas murder contradicts this liberty and abolishes the most cogent reasons for revolt. Thrust into history, which has no superior order, the rebel then is caught between the political antinomies of violence and non-violence; justice and liberty.

In principle the rebel must renounce violence, for violence is foreign to the reasons which initially motivated him. In actuality, however, he cannot turn away from the world and from history without denying the principles of his rebellion. To ignore history amounts to the same thing as denying reality. "Most certainly the rebel does not destroy the history that surrounds him; it is in terms of this that he attempts to affirm himself. But confronted with it, he feels like the artist confronted with reality; he spurns it without escaping from it" (290). An equally insoluble dilemma arises in the antinomy between justice and freedom. Absolute freedom, in maintaining the right of the strongest to dominate, confirms the reign of injustice; absolute justice, on the other hand, by tolerating no contradictions, suppresses all freedom.

XVII *The Philosophy of Limits*

According to Camus, the seemingly ineradicable opposition between the moral demands of revolt and the practical attainments of revolution must be relegated to the realm of absolutes. Such problems arise primarily because the rebel has forgotten the limitations of authentic revolt. Absolute freedom mocks at justice just as certainly as absolute justice denies freedom; but to be fruitful, the two ideas must find their limits in each other. "No man considers that his condition is free if it is not at the same time just, nor just unless it is free" (291). And the same reasoning can be applied to violence. Absolute non-violence is the negative basis of slavery and its acts of violence; systematic violence completely destroys the living community and the existence we receive from it. "To be fruitful, these two ideas must establish final limits. In history, considered as an absolute, violence finds itself legitimized; as a relative risk, it is the cause of a rupture in communication." Camus reasons that it must therefore maintain for the rebel, "its provisional character of effraction and must always be bound, if it cannot be avoided, to a personal responsibility and to an immediate risk" (292).

XVIII *The Law of Moderation*

Rebellion, then, at the same time that it brings man an awareness
of a nature which he shares with all other men also brings him an
awareness of the limits it imposes. Camus now adds the law of
moderation, a measure by which to judge all men and events, to the
values previously attained from revolt. Moderation is not the opposite of rebellion. On the contrary, rebellion in itself is moderation,
and it "demands, defends, and recreates it throughout history and
its eternal disturbances" (301). By measure or moderation, Camus
refers to that attitude of mind which opposes and is contrary to
excess of any kind. To illustrate his meaning, he points to the deification of history by modern political revolutionaries as an example of
such extremism. These revolutionaries have failed precisely because
they ignored the essential element of measure. Through their prefer-
ence for an abstract concept of man to a man of flesh and blood,
they committed themselves to a rigid dogmatism that could in no
way guarantee the achievement of human values.

Moderation, born of rebellion, can only live by rebellion. It is a perpetual
conflict, continually created and mastered by the intelligence. It does not
triumph either in the impossible or in the abyss. It finds its equilibrium
through them. Whatever we may do, excess will always keep its place in
the heart of man, in the place where solitude is found. We all carry within
us our places of exile, our crimes and our ravages. But our task is not to
unleash them on the world; it is to fight them in ourselves and in others.
(301)

There does therefore exist for man a way of acting and thinking
that is not in conflict with the principles of genuine revolt. Camus
discovers the model for present-day man to emulate in neither the
metaphysical nor the historical revolt of the post-Christian era, but
rather in the Mediterranean tradition that triumphs over abstract
ideologies by remaining constantly aware of the tension and moderation that are essential features of revolt. The Mediterranean spirit,
in conflict with German ideologies, is ever aware of man as he is
and rejects the vague promise of some far-distant Utopia in order
to assert the present grandeur of life. The true rebel chooses the
present over the future, the fate of humanity for the delusion of
power. He gives us an example of the only original rule of life today,
"to learn to live and to die, and, in order to be a man, to refuse to
be a god" (306).

XIX *Evaluation and Criticism*

Thus Camus concludes his thorough investigation of revolt in the Western world. Regardless of the faults one may find within the work, at the same time it is impossible, I think, not to be overwhelmed by the sincerity and intellectual integrity that Camus brings to it. His discussion of the movement of revolt from the pre-Christian era to modern times is profound, provocative, and essential to an understanding of our historical epoch. It is especially relevant to an American who in the 1960's is disturbed by happenings in his own country and abroad. And, as always in a discussion of Camus, the weaknesses of his reasoning—which are criticized in the conclusion of this chapter—are also strangely their strengths. Perhaps it all involves his determination to see both sides of the coin, *l'envers et l'endroit*.

As we have seen, Camus' position in *L'Homme révolté* is not fundamentally different from that of the great Western humanists who have preceded him. Although to a traditional humanist the world is not absurd and certain values are absolute, he, like Camus, also seeks to construct a valid ethical system without any recourse to *a priori* principles. Camus begins his search for values in a godless world and rather than accepting any given values, he allows man to discover these values through his own efforts. Unlike some major existentialist thinkers, Camus never denies the existence of values. To do so would completely negate one of the underlying concepts of his thought. In keeping with the development of his philosophical position up to this time, in *L'Homme révolté* he brings into question many of the phantom ideologies which prevent man from attaining his potential value and obscure him not only from himself but also from other men. In many ways, *L'Homme révolté* successfully voices a protest against the unnecessary suffering and injustice inflicted upon man by forces that menace his right to freedom and order; and in this respect it is a compelling contribution to humanistic scholarship. In substance, however, the essay is perhaps too ambitious in its aims and too ambiguous in its positive recommendations to be completely satisfying. Actually, the only practical proposal that Camus makes is to suggest a pre-Marxian form of action in keeping with the attitude of the *meurtriers délicats*, whom he extols here and in the play *Les Justes*, and this seems a somewhat meager reward for the average reader who has patiently followed the development of Camus' reasoning through some rather murky passages. It is easy to become lost in the overwhelming list of different people whom

Camus finds it necessary to mention in order to clarify his points. It has been pointed out that in a book of three hundred and seventy-eight pages, there are references to one hundred and sixty writers, ninety-six historical characters, and twenty fictional and mythical characters.[1] The fact that the list includes such powerful and diverse men as Milton, Napoleon, Christ, and Ford is frightening enough, but when one realizes that Camus devotes almost equal coverage to such major thinkers as Nietzsche, Marx, and Hegel as he does to such esoteric figures as Netchaiev, Sasanov, or Chigalev, one cannot help but be amazed that the essay retains any degree of continuity or clarity of meaning.

I do not believe it unfair to compare Camus—or for that matter, the reader of his essay—to the victim in the anecdote that Hesse quotes from Novalis in his novel *Steppenwolf*.

"Most men will not swim before they are able to." Is not that witty? Naturally, they won't swim! They are born for the solid earth, not for the water. And naturally they won't think. They are made for life, not for thought. Yes, and he who thinks, what's more, he who makes thought his business, he may go far in it, but he has bartered the solid earth for the water all the same, and one day he will drown.[2]

What I am attempting to point out is that in spite of the perfection of the prose in *L'Homme révolté*, the moral intention of the work is often confused by or even lost in the mass of ideological and historical detail which is incorporated in the essay; and like the victim in Hesse's anecdote, the reader of Camus' essay drowns in an over-abundance of exoticism.

There are other weaknesses which are equally bothersome to the person who searches for a clearly defined argument in *L'Homme révolté*. The essay has frequently been compared to *Le Mythe de Sisyphe;* and as has been previously pointed out, Camus himself refers the reader to his earlier writings on the absurd. In many ways, *L'Homme révolté* does recapitulate all of his previous work. From the earliest writings to the present essay, he depicted a world which was hazardous, uncertain, and everchanging. Over and over again from the confrontation between man's desire for coherence and the irrationality of the world, the absurd was reborn, and in Camus' plays and novels, he was able to fuse human emotion, abstract ideas, and action through his art; but this fusion that was so skillfully and effectively handled in his creative writings, here, in *L'Homme ré-volté*, becomes a puzzling and unsatisfactory technique.

The quickest way to clarify this is to contrast the opening sections of the essay with the conclusion. The main section of the book is devoted to an analysis of the unlimited revolt which dominates the history of the past two centuries and leads to the totalitarianism of today. This is the traditional concept of revolt as a protest against violence, excess, and nihilism; or to express it another way, it is the rebel's reaction to some superior power's indifference to his needs and desires as a man. In this sense revolt is a philosophical attitude, for it affirms a positive reaction to a life situation: the world is absurd and the individual reacts. However, in the conclusion of the book, revolt takes on a different meaning. It remains a protest against suffering, but it now becomes a political posture rather than an individual reaction. Revolt is specifically directed against certain dogmas of political extremism and the Marxist interpretation of history. In this part of the book, Camus limits the concept of revolt to a historical situation and makes no attempt to explain the relationship between the general philosophical meaning of the term and its narrower, political application. It is as if he saw in his own immediate experience a duplication of the initial impetus that led to man's reaction to the absurd, but he gives no reason for the shift he makes from one realm of existence to the other, from the philosophical to the political point of view.

It is also obvious to most readers that the lyrical tone of the last section of the book contrasts sharply to the clear and direct prose of the book's major portions. There are two possible reasons for the shift in style, but neither is completely satisfactory. There is no doubt that Camus' search for an ordered and harmonious society is a personal quest that can offer no set ethical system for the rebel to adhere to. In a way, to do so would eradicate the very thing that he has sought to establish. The rebel must remain free to achieve his own destiny within the limits of social necessity and not be committed to any preconceived course of action. For this reason, the mystical quality of the language and the eloquent usage of light and dark as symbols of freedom and enslavement alert the reader to the personal insight that Camus is presenting. The "Pensée de midi" is his unique poetic vision of what might be possible for man to attain in this world, and to present it in direct prose would detract from its intended impact. Yet, in spite of the nobility of Camus' plea for a moderate kind of revolt that will ensure man his freedom, individually and collectively, the glaring fact remains that the "Pensée de midi" does little to clarify the intention of the essay. For man immersed in the complexities and harsh realities of twentieth-century life, an incantation to the virtues of measure, justice, and nature offers him little to cling to. One cannot help but wonder whether Camus too did not sense the inadequacy of his conclusion and chose to couch this inadequacy in the symbol of the Mediterranean spirit.

These obviously negative aspects of the book in no way deterred either the sale or the critical acclaim accorded to it within the first year of its publication. Camus himself was proclaimed as the defender of the rights of man by French, English, and American critics alike, and more firmly than ever the reception of the book clearly established his position as one of France's most important writers. Sir Herbert Read, Waldo Frank, and Philip Toynbee were all enthusiastic in their reception of the book and praised it with great confidence as an important intellectual contribution to the understanding of man.[3] Yet, as might be anticipated, there was also strong dissenting criticism of Camus' vague ethical position and extremely personal view of history and politics. Perhaps of the many controversial discussions that were stimulated by the ideas contained in *L'Homme révolté*, the most fascinating—certainly the most publicized and most important—involved Camus himself and Jean-Paul Sartre.

XX *The Camus-Sartre Controversy*

At the origin of the open clash between Camus and Sartre, which finally broke in the August, 1952, issue of *Les Temps modernes*, is an article that appeared five months earlier in *La Nouvelle Critique*. In April, 1952, over five months after the publication of *L'Homme révolté*, Pierre Hervé, who at the time was a member of the Communist party, wrote an article in which he alleged that Camus had no interest in either colonial affairs or the dangers of nuclear warfare.[4] The entire article contained many equally ridiculous accusations and undoubtedly would have been ignored and forgotten had Jean Lebar not noted in *France-Observateur* that Hervé's criticism was quite "remarquable." For some inexplicable reason, this innocent enough adjective was misread by Camus for "belle," an adjective that would indicate Lebar's admiration for Hervé's opinions. Camus wrote an indignant letter to the *France-Observateur* in which he demanded that the paper's statement be withdrawn. There was of course no withdrawal for an error that Camus himself had made; and the incident, along with Camus' general attitude at this particular time, gave Sartre an excellent opportunity to attack Camus not only on philosophical and political grounds, but also upon grounds of personal aloofness and haughtiness. Sartre, with a deal of justification, felt that Camus had become overconscious of his role as spokesman for the French intellectual and in a scathing remark commented: "Tell me, Camus, by what strange miracle can one not criticise your books without depriving humanity of its reasons for living?" [5]

This personal taunting tone unfortunately runs through a great deal of the discussion of Camus' ideas by both Sartre and his disciple Francis Jeanson. In May, 1952, Jeanson published a long and highly critical review of *L'Homme révolté* in *Les Temps modernes* in which he primarily accused Camus of failing to face today's real issues. Jeanson maintained that Camus sought in *L'Homme révolté* to remain outside of history, that he ignored the struggles of men in favor of metaphysical concepts, and that through his emphasis upon the crimes committed by revolutionaries and his attack upon Marxism and Stalinism, he allied himself with the smug bourgeoisie and reinforced the ideas it wished to hear.

Three months after the Jeanson article appeared, *Les Temps modernes* published a sixteen-page letter of self-defense written by Camus at Sartre's invitation. In the same issue were also published letters of reply from both Sartre and Jeanson. The actual debate between the men centered around their disagreement concerning the political position of a left-wing intellectual. Sartre maintained that only through support of the Communist party, through an active attempt to orient it where possible from within, could an honest course of political action be followed. Although he in no way found the party the perfect answer to the problems of the working class, he insisted that, "In order to deserve the right to influence men who struggle, one must start by participating in their battle. One must start by accepting a lot of things, if one wants to attempt to change a few." [6] Camus challenged the efficacy of Sartre's position and called for a new orientation of leftist-intellectual thought through his analysis of the degradation of the ideologies of the French Revolution and the Communist party, and he further asserted that no honest movement could have anything at all to do with Stalinism.

Regardless of the political issues debated by the two men, the argument ultimately concerned the philosophical differences between them. Sartre refuses any prior human nature and sees man as the sum of all his acts. Man is in history and through his actions in time he creates values which can come into being only through an active engagement in political activity. Although Camus agrees with Sartre that man exists physically in history, at the same time he also believes that man can transcend history by his participation in what he chooses to call the human spirit. In his letter to Sartre, he draws attention to a basic contradiction in Sartre's position:

Only prophetic Marxism (or a philosophy of eternity), could justify the pure and simple rejection of my thesis, but how can such views be upheld in your magazine without contradiction? Because, after all, if there is no human end that can be made into a norm of value, how can history have a definable meaning? On the other hand, if history has meaning why shouldn't man make of it his end? [7]

These questions actually remained unanswered. Sartre replied to Camus that, "Man participates in history in order to pursue the eternal. He uncovers universal values in the concrete action which he performs with a specific purpose in view." But his statement does little to clarify the issue at hand. In fact, as John Cruickshank points out, Sartre's use of such concepts as "the eternal" and "universal values" seems to approach a position amazingly close to Camus'.[8]

Without delving into the complexities of the discussion between the two men,[9] perhaps the most disappointing aspect of the quarrel is that neither Camus nor Sartre, who were both sincerely involved in a search for human betterment, could establish a common ground on which to meet. Certainly neither won the argument. There is something humanly compelling in Sartre's restless desire to improve the condition of man through immediate direct action, regardless of the obvious pitfalls his chosen course of action may contain. On the other hand, one must admire Camus' honest attempt to do something that Sartre has never done. In *L'Homme révolté*, because he felt intellectually responsible for his commitments, he endeavored to account for the position he took toward the political ideologies of our time. There is little doubt that Camus' position is the more idealistic of the two—a patient search for values is always a logically superior method of action to that of a fatal comitment to a militant ideology—however, given the twentieth-century situation, the question remains unanswered whether or not a man can take time daily to reexamine and to redefine his position.

XXI *Conclusion*

The intellectual controversy that arose following the publication of *L'Homme révolté* monopolized Camus' time well into 1952, and usurped energy that could perhaps have been profitably spent in more creative ways. For Camus, however, there could have been no escape from his involvement. Throughout his entire career, he was constantly and passionately involved not only with what he thought and what he wrote but also with the way people received and reacted to his ideas. Unlike some writers and philosophers, Camus could never divorce himself from his writings. Whether he wrote of death, of longing, or of revolt, it was always his death, his longing, or his revolt about which he spoke. This intense and often painful relationship between the man and his work is both a weakness and a strength. It is a weakness, because the personal and poetic qualities of his writings are frequently difficult to pinpoint and often—as in the "Pensée de midi"—so personal as to defy criticism. Conversely, the personal diligence with which he develops his experiences into a philosophy is so honest and so moving an experience that the reader is forced to work with Camus from step to step in his discussion until they both attain a conclusion—now far removed from the initial personal experience—that is both logically and humanly tenable. Sartre, too, in spite of their quarrel, must have felt some of this same fascination for Camus when he wrote in his tribute to him,

That man on the move questioned us, was himself a question seeking its reply; he lived *in the middle of a long life;* for us, for him, for the men who maintain order and for those who reject it, it was important for him to break his silence, for him to decide, for him to conclude.[10]

CHAPTER 8

The Other Side of the Coin

I 1951–1956

NINETEEN hundred and fifty-six, the year of the publication of
La Chute, marks Camus' return to imaginative writing. But
the years between 1951 and 1956 were not silent ones. There are
the essays that make up the collections of *Actuelles II* and *L'Eté;*
there are the translations, adaptations, and productions of plays by
Calderón de la Barca, Pierre Larivey, Dino Buzzati, Faulkner, and
Dostoevski; and there are the prefaces to the works of Oscar Wilde
and Martin du Gard. Although many may have wondered if Camus
had not lost himself in the mass of ideological and historical detail
incorporated in *L'Homme révolté*, the works that were published
during this time indicated that he was consciously limiting his
literary activities to a personal and public clarification of what he
had already written. The secret, inner conflict that he had to resolve
before he could again assert his powers as a creative writer involved
his own understanding of his role as an artist in the twentieth century. He had to free himself from doctrinaire imperatives, from
political commitment, and to return to his initial conviction that "the
supreme aim of art is to confound all judges, to abolish all accusations, and to justify everything, life and mankind, in a light which
is the light of beauty only because it is the light of truth."[1]

II L'Eté

To rediscover his own "light of beauty," Camus had first to rediscover himself. *L'Homme révolté* marked a stage in his thought
beyond which it was difficult for him to progress in the same direction. He now needed to know if he could find again the source of
joy, love, and light that originally had protected him against despair.
The truth of his pilgrimage to self-understanding is expressed in the

eight lyrical essays published under the title of *L'Eté*. These essays, written between 1939 and 1951, are dominated by an emphasis on beauty, happiness, and art that characterized his earlier writings, and they represent Camus' return to a lyrical meditation on the richness of the universe and the happiness of life that is reminiscent of *L'Envers et l'endroit* and *Noces*. The crisis of the war had passed, and Camus felt that he could temporarily at least reject the arid arguments of political controversy that held out vague promises for the future and take up his search for fulfillment of a life firmly rooted in the present moment. In the preface to the 1957 edition of *L'Envers et l'endroit*, he declared his intention to begin all over again, to go all the way back to this first work which contained all the contradictions, the ambiguities, the two facets of light and shadow, innocence and guilt which characterized his world of life and creativity. Given the characteristics of Camus' manner of gradually developing his own philosophical position, it is not at all surprising that after the intense questioning that underlies the thought of *L'Homme révolté*, he should again return to his initial artistic impulse. The investigations of the political evils of his epoch left little room for the impassioned appreciation of life that runs through his less didactic writings.

III   La Chute

We have seen that each stage in his thought is a struggle toward a certain intellectual grasp of life. Unlike a systematic philosopher such as Sartre, Camus felt his way into his philosophy by first examining an aspect of experience on the personal level and then expanding this personal experience into a universal truth that would better illuminate the human condition. Thus, just as *L'Etranger* foreshadowed a philosophical position which was further clarified in *Le Mythe de Sisyphe*, the idea of limits, inherent in *La Peste* but not fully developed until *L'Homme révolté*, corrected and defined the initial position. It is from this deliberate self-limitation to a unified idea that Camus draws his power as an artist and a thinker. It is a complex thought process that allows him to experiment, to limit, and eventually to evolve a philosophical position that without ever negating the initial impulse is constantly correcting and refining it. In his essay "L'Artiste et son temps," he said that "the aim of art is . . . first to understand." [2] It was his desire to understand the complexities of life that led him through the manifold stages of his developing thought, and it is exactly this same characteristic that compelled him to write the most controversial of all his books, *La Chute*.

In a fashion reminiscent of Coleridge's Ancient Mariner, Jean-Baptiste Clamence, the monologist of *La Chute*, awaits his opportunity to engage a stranger in conversation and to confess to him his past crimes and weaknesses. His tale is an engaging one, told with cynical wit and scheming complicity. As his narration progresses through six short sections, the reader soon realizes that it is he whom Clamence has chosen as his audience. Clamence begins telling his weird story in a cheap waterfront bar called the Mexico City, located in the slum section of Amsterdam. At one time he had been an envied and highly esteemed Parisian lawyer. He had defended the poor and the victimized, and enjoyed the pleasure of knowing that he was on the right side. He was good looking, an excellent dancer, a marvelous conversationalist, a generous and courteous man. He was, in other words, a ·pillar of bourgeois society; and everything seemed to tell him that the happiness he so completely enjoyed was authorized "by some higher decree" (29).[3] Then one night as he was returning quite late from a visit to one of his mistresses, something happened which shattered his moral complacency and self-esteem. As he crossed the Seine on the Pont Royal, he passed a slim young woman dressed in black. She was leaning over the bridge railing and staring into the river. After he had gone on some fifty yards he heard the sound "of a body striking the water" (70). He stopped, listened, and heard a cry repeated several times. He stood motionless; then went away, but he was never permitted to forget the suicide he might have prevented. The memory of this moment of cowardice was kept alive by a mysterious sound of laughter which had "come from nowhere, unless from the water" (39).

From this time on, Clamence began to see within himself the vanity, "the handsome wax figure," the emptiness that he was. As he progressed from memory to memory, he gradually discovered that his former good deeds had been done only for the sake of popular approval. He could remember no moral or courteous act that he had performed when there were no witnesses to applaud his actions. Overcome by the hollowness of his existence, he decided to immunize himself against the laughter he felt by immersing himself in various forms of debauchery. One day, however, aboard a ship, he perceived a black speck on the steel-gray ocean that reminded him of a drowning person. It was then that he realized that he could not escape the cry which had sounded over the Seine many years before, that he had to submit and admit to a guilt that would await him "on seas and rivers, everywhere" (108). Consciously aware of the "fundamental duplicity of the human being" (84) and the fact that "the keenest of human torments is to be judged without a law" (117), Clamence dedicated himself to the function of judge-penitent. From that moment of decision onward, he made endurable the duplicity he had discovered by persuading his listeners that they too were guilty of the same amazing and horrifying acts. Only by judging himself could he escape the judgment of others, and only through his own confession could the image he creates of himself "become a mirror" to his contemporaries and proclaim the inescapable guilt of all men:

Covered with ashes, tearing my hair, my face scored by clawing, but with piercing eyes, I stand before all humanity recapitulating my shames without losing sight of the effect I am producing, and saying: "I was the lowest of the low." Then imperceptibly I pass from the "I" to the "we." When I get to "This is what we are," the trick has been played and I can tell them off. I am like them, to be sure; we are in the soup together. However, I have a superiority in that I know it and this gives me the right to speak. You see the advantage, I am sure. The more I accuse myself, the more I have a right to judge you. Even better, I provoke you into judging yourself, and this relieves me of that much of the burden. (140)

IV Relationship of La Chute *to Camus' Other Works*

I am sure that this rather cursory outline of the action of *La Chute* alerts the reader to an emphasis upon certain aspects of human behavior that have not heretofore been investigated by Camus. In all his writings, from *L'Envers et l'endroit* to *L'Homme révolté*, there has been an underlying assumption of human innocence. Camus has consistently defended the innocence of man against those ideologies and theologies which attempt to corrupt this innocence and treat him as if guilty. In *Le Mythe de Sisyphe*, in *L'Homme révolté*, as well as in the more imaginative writings, evil was always considered a force outside of man. In *L'Etranger*, the structure of society was seen to be more at fault than Meursault; in *La Peste*, man in general was presented as the innocent victim of events; much of the critical commentary surrounding *L'Homme révolté* resulted from Camus' oversimplification of the problem of evil. There he blamed the crimes committed in the name of Communism upon the philosopher Hegel. Realizing the one-sided aspect of his argument up to this time, Camus seeks to correct his reasoning in *La Chute*. If, as he

previously argued, man is innocent, then the natural assumption is
that all men are innocent. The laws of logic dictate that if all men
are innocent, there can be no man-created evil which they would
be compelled to resist. Obviously, evil does exist, and men exist who
create the conditions against which the rebel revolts. Camus reasons
in a way similar to Sartre's that although the subjective "I" views
itself as innocent, the day must arrive when this subjective "I" per-
ceives another "I" who also considers itself as innocent. Up to the
moment of confrontation between the "I" and an "other," it is possible to speak of evil as outside the self or in "others," but after the
confrontation the "I" becomes aware that to the "others" he is an
"other." The "I" then recognizes both his subjective innocence and
his objective guilt. It is this double nature of man—certainly not
an original concept—that Camus now turns to and investigates in
La Chute. His concern with the guilty evildoer, Jean-Baptiste
Clamence, as opposed to the innocent rebels who up to this time
have been his central concern, represents a turning point in his
thought and a progression to a more complete, if less optimistic,
understanding of the nature of man.

V *Interpretation*

There are countless references to man's duality throughout the
book. The title itself suggests that there was a state of innocence
before the fall into the Hell of present-day Amsterdam. The city is
used as an artistic device in much the same way that Oran was
employed in *La Peste*. Here, in contrast to the blazing sunlight of
Oran, but nonetheless reflecting the same artistic intent, the rain
and mist of Amsterdam create a psychological atmosphere that
emphasizes the uncertainty of the ideas expressed in the book. At
Amsterdam, the Zuider Zee of which no one knows "where it begins
or ends" (97); the canals with their "stagnant waters" and "smell
of dead leaves"; and even the people who "are here and elsewhere"
all reflect the tone of the book: the modern hell of ambiguity in which
it is impossible to distinguish between guilt and innocence. Unlike
the innocent rebels of *L'Etranger* and *La Peste*, there is no clarity
for the people of this northern world, no blending into a perfect
harmony with life. They can distinguish neither on the physical nor
on the moral level. Their life is not one of blindness, but one of
unclarity. In much the same way that we might awkwardly stumble
and fall in foggy half-light, the men of this modern world cannot
intellectually perceive their ideals. Theirs is an existence of eternal

doubt, distrust, and fall. There is no doctrine of redemption, no law to guide them; their fall is not the Christian fall from innocence, but rather a fall from innocence that is self-inflicted without any reference to law. Clamence says that "He who clings to a law does not fear the judgment that reinstates him in an order he believes in. But the keenest of human torments is to be judged without a law" (117).

There are two closely related episodes that serve a double purpose. They both clarify the keen suffering that Clamence inflicts upon himself and they also help to define Camus' special use of the word "fall." We are already familiar with the first crucial event that shattered Clamence's Parisian paradise. Although unaware of it at the time, the evening that he ignored the cry of the slim young woman on the Pont Royal ushered in his state of guilt. The second central moment, derived from the first, took place two or three years later, and again occurred on a bridge over the River Seine. Clamence was happy within himself. He had had a good day and was enjoying a vast feeling of power and completion. At the very moment he was about to light "a cigarette of satisfaction" (39), a laugh burst out behind him. He wheeled around suddenly but no one was there. He turned back and again heard the laughter a little farther off "as if it were going downstream" (39).

This laugh which Clamence "believed" he heard is the great event which shattered his complacency, and even the most casual reader notices similarities between this event and the earlier one. There are the similarities of the setting, of the scene, and of the time: a bridge, deserted or becoming so, darkness, autumn. In both instances, Clamence is alone, satisfied and happy. During the event, there is the perception of a noise—a laugh, a cry—behind Clamence, from an unknown source—an invisible person, an unidentified woman—a noise repeated, still from behind him, which floats down the river. After the event, the immediate reaction of Clamence in both cases is a kind of immobilization or paralysis, followed by parallel nervous reactions of skin and heart. As if in a dream, the second experience is a distortion at the subconscious level of the former one: the suicide which Clamence thought he had forgotten was essentially reproduced for him when he stumbled upon the set of circumstances with which he subconsciously associated it.

It is at this time that Clamence must come to conscious awareness of his previous action. He can no longer ignore his responsibility as a human being. Although he endeavors to lose himself in debauchery and to escape his guilt, he cannot. He goes through a long period of revolt against the implications of the laugh, but when he has come to think that his efforts to avoid responsibility have finally succeeded; when, through debauchery, the last phase of his revolt, he has reached a state of existence so foggy that "the laughter became so muffled that eventually [he] ceased to notice it" (106), he is caught off guard by the black speck he saw on the steel-gray ocean and is forced to acknowledge the event of the suicide and to resign himself to his guilt. He must finally admit that he had taken upon himself the responsibility for his actions the evening he chose to ignore the woman on the bridge. Up to that time he had acted in accord with a set of imposed values—values established by the society he lived in. But on that particular evening he was alone, there was no witness to applaud his acts, and on that evening when he ignored the plaint of the drowning woman, he chose himself above the virtuous code he had been following. It was at that time that he placed complete responsibility upon himself and rejected his Parisian paradise. The total implication of the decision is not realized until the second bridge episode with its similar conditions. From this point onward, Clamence moved toward full consciousness. It is an intriguing psychological mesh that Camus entangles him in. Once the initial act has been committed, Clamence cannot ever again regain his former state of innocence. It might be argued that his fall into the awareness of his freedom and responsibility is a fall into a better state than his earlier unconscious innocence, but the fact remains that the condition has changed and that Clamence finds it almost impossible to face himself and to bring his personal life into some sort of accord with his understanding of himself and the world.

The fall then for Camus is a fall into an awareness of the truth—the truth of man's position in the twentieth century. In this book, as in the others we have discussed, there is a biting criticism of the man-controlled laws that govern and judge human behavior; and because of this factor, the early Clamence has much in common with Camus' other heroes. He personifies that very aspect of society which sat in judgment upon Meursault. Clamence, before his fall, was the most eloquent pleader for the accused and oppressed. He was the example par excellence of those formidable bourgeois who defend the letter of the law without ever questioning its morality. But it is Clamence after his fall who is most interesting to us, and it is in his state of guilt that his comparison to Meursault becomes most meaningful.

The difference between Clamence and Meursault here is that Clamence is guilty of an act, unjudged and untried by society, whereas Meursault was tried and judged for an act which in reality he did not commit. In the case of Meursault, society is willing to overlook the fact that he murdered an Arab, but it is at the same time unwilling to ignore Meursault's seeming indifference at his mother's wake. It is for his crime of being an outsider to his social milieu that Meursault is finally sentenced to death, but in his final moments of life Meursault is granted the luxury of personal happiness. He is able to discover and enjoy an inner satisfaction that Clamence never achieves. Clamence's crime, legally, is no crime at all; but his awareness of his guilt, his failure to measure up to human expectations, is acute enough to plague his conscience and to force him into a state of self-inflicted punishment. The contrast might be expressed in still another way. Through his trial, Meursault is awakened to life and the splendors of the universe, whereas Clamence, through his self-imposed judgment, is awakened to an awareness of his other self and the Hell of modern man. In both situations, Camus seems to be saying that in order to achieve any measure of human happiness, the individual, aware of his freedom, must accept total responsibility for all his actions.

In a less dramatic sense, the early Clamence also resembles Dr. Rieux. He, like Rieux, acts in accordance with the laws of his society and, from one point of view, Clamence can be defended as a benefactor and healer of mankind. He helps the poor, aids the crippled, defends the unfortunate. He, again like Rieux, subscribes to no orthodox religion, and his own estimation of himself as "fully and simply a man" echoes Rieux's interest in "being a man." Although Rieux has none of the haughtiness of Clamence, little of his conceit, they do share a certain desire to do a job well within the framework of an absurd universe. As many critics have suggested, *La Chute* may be read as Camus' own criticism of the implied innocence of man implicit in *La Peste*, for until Clamence became fully conscious of his impure motives, he had been living as a legal equivalent of Dr. Rieux.

However, regardless of the similarities between Clamence and the earlier heroes, there is one element that clearly distinguishes him from his literary ancestors. Clamence is overwhelmingly dissatisfied with his role in the universe. He discovers neither the splendors of Meursault's world nor the magnificence of Rieux's men. He only discovers his own middle-class Hell with its "streets filled with shop signs and no way of explaining one-self" (47). He is acutely aware of his own and of mankind's shortcomings, but he is able to do nothing about them. In a striking way Clamence is not evil incarnate (as we are apt first to interpret him), but rather he is the incarnation of twentieth-century hopes and joys gone astray.

Here again, Camus has taken an individual experience and expanded it to reflect a universal truth. Clamence as "the image of all and of no one" is the concrete example of the suffering of all men within twentieth-century bourgeois society. There are no values for him to catch hold of. The wars and the events following the wars have left little of enduring worth for mankind. Clamence cannot find the quiet joys that Meursault and Rieux found so enduring. He knows nothing of the friendship that Rieux experienced with Tarrou. He only knows that the "earth is dark, . . . the coffin thick, and the shroud opaque" (74). He can find no certainty in anything. Yet, he admits that he loves life, and that fact is not only, as he says, his "real weakness," but it is also his real tragedy.

Clamence is truly the man adrift. He is conscious of his own weaknesses and in turn he bears the weight of the painful consciousness of the weakness of the entire world. He is a man who that night on the bridge forsook his innocence, his virtue, and became free. But his freedom by his own admission is unbearable. And Camus seems to be saying that twentieth-century man is in much the same position as Clamence. Neither can find a law to cling to that will regain the lost paradise for him. They both suffer the consequences of their moment in history, and in order to make life have some meaning they surmount the agony of moral uncertainty and the horror of freedom by finding other men who share their guilt. Clamence is modern man, with all his frustrating search for lost values, who in lieu of these values has set himself up as a god. Only by judging others and making them aware of their guilt can he in some small way at least endure his freedom. Clamence tells us that "on the bridges of Paris I . . . learned that I was afraid of freedom" (136). The fact that he chose his freedom the night he ignored the woman on the bridge in no way makes the burden of this freedom any easier to bear. In order to bear life at all, he must find others to share his guilt, for only by judging others can he lighten the weight of the judgment he has placed upon himself.

VI *Comparison of Clamence to Meursault and Rieux*
Seen in this manner, Clamence takes his place alongside of

Meursault, Rieux, and Camus' other characters to present a composite picture of modern man. Clamence the lawyer could as easily be Clamence the doctor, the teacher, the philosopher. His function, like that of many learned and intellectual people, is to perceive the dangers of present-day society, to point out these dangers, and to offer a few positive suggestions to better the situation. Clamence proceeds a step further than most twentieth-century intellectuals in that he does insert the idea of some distant hope. The faint hope that Clamence offers to modern man is the belief that through self-judgment, he can attain an understanding, prepare the way to the rediscovery of an old innocence and a new law that will protect this innocence. By living through the Hell that is his, he never loses sight of the islands that hold out the promise of a brighter future, the islands of innocence and redemption. Amsterdam is, after all, the "last circle," the densest and darkest of Hell; and although Clamence has "learned to be satisfied with understanding," the implied hope exists that the rest of mankind may someday progress beyond satisfaction to an attainment of "the light, the mornings, the holy innocence of those who forgive themselves" (145).

The duality that is the essence of Clamence's character, indeed the very nature of man, is underlined by almost every sentence of *La Chute* and carries over to the reader's reaction to this strange but familiar confession. Many critics have seen Camus' ideas directly reflected in Clamence's judgments, and there is no doubt that Camus used much of his own experience in creating his modern-day John the Baptist. Camus' own personal charm, his consciousness of the elegance of language, his opposition to judges and unfeeling legalism, his concern with religion and politics are all reflected in his portrayal of Clamence. But in spite of these obvious connections between the author and his creation, the book remains one of the least revealing confessions ever written. According to Clamence, "authors of confessions write especially to avoid confessing, to tell nothing of what they know" (120); and his statement in many ways serves as an astute judgment on those critics who strain to find a too exact parallel between Camus and Clamence.

In his portrait of Clamence, Camus is not so much interested in creating an individual as he is in using a particular individual as the embodiment of an idea. Clamence shares those characteristics of Camus' that at one time or another everyone in his moral self-consciousness shares with him. Ours is, after all, the century of the exploration of the "I," the epoch that finds it difficult to love, the age in which communication is a one-sided authoritarian affair. *La Chute* further suggests that it is a time of inaction, in which "words, words, words" resound against a cold, empty backdrop of gray. Ours is also an era that in its emphasis on the "I, I, I" leads the individual in his most despondent moments to be seduced into agreement with Clamence's desire "to block the door of the closed little universe of which I am the king, the pope, and the judge" (128). All these ideas, generally stated here but more precisely discussed in the text of *La Chute*, must be common property to the majority of thinking men in our time. If not, the effectiveness of the book would be lost to all but those few who have an intimate knowledge of Camus' biography. Camus, himself aware of the limiting aspect that a strictly biographical interpretation would impose upon *La Chute*, prefaced the English edition with the following quotation from Lermontov:

Some were dreadfully insulted, and quite seriously, to have held up as a model such an immoral character as *A Hero of Our Time;* others shrewdly noticed that the author had portrayed himself and his acquaintances. . . . *A Hero of Our Time*, gentlemen, is in fact a portrait, but not of an individual; it is the aggregate of the vices of our whole generation in their fullest expression.

Beyond the obvious biographical and fictional parallels between Clamence and Camus, the reader totally ignorant of Camus' personal life and thought is drawn into a much broader and more significant portrayal than that of an individual man in the 1950's. Clamence is not only by his own admission the mirror of "all and of no one." The tragedy of a Clamence, of the man without traditional values, who is in desperate search of something—almost anything—that will give meaning to his life, is the tragedy of many men of this century. The pat answers, indifferently meted out by the church and the state, really offer no solace once challenged. Within a world that lives in constant fear of total destruction, man needs an answer that can be tangibly illustrated. Meursault found this answer in the warmth and beauties of the Mediterranean sun. He needed nothing beyond the present moment and the promise of a never-ending succession of moments. Rieux found his answer in the inherent dignity of man. But for Clamence, placed actually in the same bourgeois, bureaucratic world, there is no universal splendor, no human warmth. He is one of the less fortunate who cannot find any satisfaction. He longs for his lost innocence but is aware of his guilt and cannot find any noble solution to his dilemma. This almost totally pessimistic portrayal of modern man as a creature of duplicity whose bad faith can destroy even his best intentions does not negate the truths of Camus' earlier writings any more than *La Peste* negated the absurd universe of *L'Etranger*. What man can accomplish against collective evil is one thing; what he can do to control the evil of an individual human conscience is quite another.

In *La Chute*, Camus has put his finger on the anguish of an age, and he offers no easy solution to this anguish. It is a truth, as real and as powerful as the truth of absurdity and revolt, and in its own way it contributes powerfully to the understanding of modern man. Camus no longer wished to see white and black, innocence and guilt, each concealing the other. He wished not only to place them side by side but to mingle them, to see the *l'envers et l'endroit*, the exile and the kingdom as one. As Clamence warns us, his confession is only addressed to the Sadducee in us, the part of each individual that clings to the status quo, to the letter of the law. In Camus' next major writing, *L'Exil et le Royaume*, he sustains rather than negates the essentially enigmatic nature of man, and in this collection of short stories he portrays men and women who live with but do not torture themselves about the mixture of guilt and innocence, the multiple faces of man.

CHAPTER 9

The Kingdom of Man

I L'Exil et le Royaume

L'EXIL *et le Royaume*, Camus' last published creative work, is perhaps his most perfectly finished work of art. In this collection of six short stories, he reveals not only his ability to illuminate "the problems of the human conscience in our times," but also his poetic power to capture, assemble, and restore the "unique throbbing of life." In no other work since *Noces* has he displayed so openly his personal and inimitable stamp: his Algerian birth, his appreciation for the fullness of joy in the physical life, his understanding of human warmth and compassion, and his suffering from separation and loneliness. The power of these six tales to convey the diversity of life and the wealth of man do much to cancel out the bittersweet pessimism of *La Chute*. The long, dreary evenings and the damp, cold winters of Clamence's Europe are momentarily forgotten as Camus writes of his longings for the world where contradictions will be resolved.

These brilliant stories of men and women in search of an inner kingdom where they can forget their spiritual exile reveal little about the evolution of Camus' ideas, but they tell us much about his own longings for an Algeria that he could never forget. In Paris at this time he was not only in real exile from his native land; but by the force of circumstances in post-war France, he was also intellectually separated from his own political beliefs and ideals. His private problems as an artist, committed both to his art and his world, are handled with superior deftness in these simple tales of men and women seen in differing moments of human experience. A wife leaves her husband's bed to give herself completely to the desert night; a missionary, loving the savages who have tortured him, teaches us the true meaning of intolerance; a melancholy workman fails to make contact with other men and longs for the happier days of his lost youth; a French schoolmaster, in his desire to do good, suffers from a misunderstanding and is hated for a deed of love; an artist is caught between the demands of society and the pursuit of his art; and an engineer finds his place among men by learning to share their struggles.

In each of these stories, Camus concentrates upon the qualities and problems of an ordinary man in a particular situation. Although these people suffer sharply from man's metaphysical fate and his daily misery, they do not incarnate abstract ideas in the manner of Meursault, Rieux, or Clamence. They are members of ordinary humanity who neither withdraw from the facts of life nor sacrifice themselves to them. Without ever quite forgetting their own individuality, they are able to join other men by sharing their struggles. The entire human being is found again as Camus rediscovers his joys in the fruits and flowers of the land; in the union of land and sea; in the coming together of two strong young bodies; in the inundation of his whole being with the loveliness of earth; in the power of man to endure.

II *The Central Theme*

The unity of the collection is conveyed by Camus' emphasis on the theme of separation that all the stories reflect, but at the same time each piece remains a separate work of art. More than any other single device, it is the stylistic excellence, the magnificent diversity of expression, that Camus employs as he moves from one story to another, that sets the entire volume apart and makes it unique. The descriptive language of "La Femme adultère" and "La Pierre qui pousse"; the stream-of-consciousness technique of "Le Renégat"; the humor and irony of "Jonas"; the directness of "Les Muets" and "L'Hôte" provide a showcase for Camus' artistic virtuosity. From his combination of an active creative power with a skilled mastery of language, characters emerge that "by some miracle of art . . . continue to live, while ceasing to be mortal . . ." (257).[1]

III *Camus' Theory of Art*

The discussion of style in *L'Homme révolté* in many ways helps the critic to understand Camus' exact intentions in *L'Exil et le Royaume*. The section of *L'Homme révolté* that I am referring to develops his theory of art in general, with specific emphasis placed upon the art of the novel. Although Camus describes *L'Etranger* and *La Chute* as "récits" and *La Peste* as a "chronique," all his works clearly illustrate the stylization of reality that he found characteristic of the greatest art. In *L'Homme révolté,* he argues that all artists in one way or another revolt against the natural formlessness of life and reconstruct the world according to their own plan. By extracting from natural disorder a unity which is more satisfying to the mind and the heart, the artist restores form to the general confusion of reality. The artist's arrangement and selection of details from reality in no way implies his failure to understand and to acknowledge the fact of total reality, for to ignore it would end in a mediocre effort to escape it rather than to clarify and order it. Quite the opposite of rejecting the real world, the world of art is the same world of suffering, illusion, and love that we know; this world is neither more beautiful nor more enlightening than ours; the heroes speak our language and have our weaknesses and strengths. But the artist, through his exercise of selectivity, creates out of the chaotic world known to us a world that is peopled by men and women who complete things which we in the real world cannot ever consummate. The events which make up our lives are without pattern, and it is the rare individual who can give life the fixed and irredeemable quality which he longs for. But through the controlling hand of the artist, the fictional character is allowed to pursue his destiny to the end without the interruptions that a real-life situation imposes. According to Camus, it is this factor of completion which gives art its meaning and its appeal. Although we fully realize that the worlds of the Julien Sorels or the Princes of Clèves are not our worlds, we can identify with them; and because of the order that their lives contain, we can fulfill our esthetic need for a unified world. Thus, the imaginary world that the artist creates from the rectification of the actual world surpasses our world, for it gives to us the "alleviating form and limits" which we vainly pursue in our own lives.

According to Camus, it is within this sealed world, created by the artist, that "man can reign and have knowledge at last" (255). Through the artist's isolation of his subject matter in time and space, he unifies and reconstructs the world according to his plan and can "stylize and imprison one significant expression" in order to illuminate one aspect of the "infinite variety of human attitudes" (256). Although the world in all its manifestations is valid territory for artistic exploration, in his creation of the imaginary world, the artist's rejection of reality cannot be total; for unity is not communicable in the purely imaginable. The true artist uses reality with "all its warmth and its blood" and adds something which transfigures it.

That which he retains of reality declares the artist's degree of consent given to at least one part of it. "This correction which the artist imposes by his language and by a redistribution of elements derived from reality, is called style and gives the recreated universe its unity and its boundaries" (269).

If we think back at this point to the characters that make up Camus' private universe, we realize that the general movement of his own artistic attitude has been in the direction of esthetic unity. In his search for man's destiny, he has consistently refused the world as he found it and sought to create a unified world that man could understand. Through his description of a closed universe, he has allowed all of the characters from Meursault through Rieux to Clamence the luxury of attempting to create a substitute universe which possesses the unity they demand. They neither renounce nor reject the actual world, but they refuse the disorder they find in it and fabricate order and unity out of the chaos that surrounds them.

I said that this aspect of Camus' art is consistent; yet it is necessary briefly to distinguish between the underlying philosophical intent of his earlier and later writings. The juxtaposition of man and his need for unity and the world and its disunity remains the same in the absurd writings and the works following the development of Camus' philosophy of limits. The difference, however—and it is an essential one—is one of broad philosophical implications. In the absurd experiment, Camus felt no compulsion to construct a world of order and value, for any devised system of unity was condemned to die along with the man who created it. In the philosophy of limits, however, man is called upon to recreate the world in spite of his death; for it is only through his recognition of the power of the individual to effect a positive change in the values of the world that man can hope for any degree of human happiness. In very simple terminology, it is Sisyphus' recognition that he is not alone in an indifferent universe.

These ideas are essential not only to the narrative art of *L'Exil et le Royaume*, but also to an understanding of the motivation of the characters themselves. In their search for an earthly kingdom, each of them is acutely aware of his own position in the world. These are very human stories that focus upon a given man in a particular moment and endeavor to express his quest to find value in a world of constant change and endless contradiction. In a sense, each of them knows that he will never achieve final triumph in his struggle with the world; but he also knows that for his life to have any meaning, he must follow the only course open to him and create his own values within the limits imposed upon him by his own nature. They all echo Camus' own statement in *L'Homme révolté* that, ". . . on my self alone rests the common dignity which I cannot allow to be debased either in myself or others."

IV *"La Femme adultère"*

"La Femme adultère" is the first story of the collection and the only one to have a woman as its central figure. Janine, the middle-aged protagonist, accompanies her husband on a business trip among the villages of southern Algeria. There in the vastness and silence of the desert, she is strangely attracted to the nomadic tribesmen who "since the beginning of time . . . had been ceaselessly trudging, possessing nothing but serving no one, poverty-stricken but free lords of a strange kingdom" (24).[2] Contemplating her own life, its lost youth, her cheated heart, she identifies the nomadic kingdom as her own: a kingdom that had been promised to her from all time. In her own heart she finds ". . . something of which, though it had always been lacking, she had never been aware of until now" (23). She realizes in this vast expanse of territory, where life is suspended and time stands still, that she must instantly seize this "something" or never again know its meaning.

That evening she leaves her bed to escape into the night and to re-capture the lost kingdom of her youth. In the rapturous yielding of her body to the "benign indifference of the universe," she consum-mates her adultery with the forces of nature. In an extraordinarily beautiful passage, Camus describes Janine's complete surrender of her body to the "sky in movement."

Not a breath, not a sound—except at intervals the muffled crackling of stones that the cold was reducing to sand—disturbed the solitude and silence surrounding Janine. After a moment, however, it seemed to her that the sky above her was moving in a sort of slow gyration. In the vast reaches of the dry, cold night, thousands of stars were constantly appear-ing, and their sparkling icicles, loosened at once, began to slip gradually toward the horizon. Janine could not tear herself away from contemplating those drifting flares. She was turning with them, and the apparently sta-tionary progress little by little identified her with the core of her being, where cold and desire were now vying with each other. Before her the stars were falling one by one and being snuffed out among the stones of the desert, and each time Janine opened a little more to the night. Breath-ing deeply, she forgot the cold, the dead weight of others, the craziness or

The Kingdom of Man

stuffiness of life, the long anguish of living and dying. After so many years of mad, aimless fleeing from fear, she had come to a stop at last. At the same time, she seemed to recover her roots and the sap again rose in her body, which had ceased trembling. Her whole belly pressed against the parapet as she strained toward the moving sky; she was merely waiting for her fluttering heart to calm down and establish silence within her. The last stars of the constellations dropped their clusters a little lower on the desert horizon and became still. Then, with unbearable gentleness, the water of night began to fill Janine, drowned the cold, rose gradually from the hidden core of her being and overflowed in wave after wave, rising up even to her mouth full of moans. The next moment, the whole sky stretched out over her, fallen on her back on the cold earth. (32–33)

Later, Janine returns to her sterile marriage bed, her exile. For only a brief moment, she has been able to escape the coldness and loneliness of her life and be totally at one with the mystery of the universe.

In this story, along with the others of the collection, the human experience is neither analyzed nor agonized over. In a poetic, rather than a political or philosophical sense, these tales reflect Camus' statement in *L'Homme révolté* that, "Real generosity towards the future lies in giving all to the present" (271). The heroism of these characters is exactly their ability to feel and act upon situations with a grandeur that Camus has consistently found to be an essential aspect of man.

V *"Le Renégat"*

"Le Renégat," the second story of the collection, tells how man's will to self-expression can be easily misdirected. This story, significantly subtitled "Un Esprit confus," tells of a French missionary who has taken upon himself the impossible task of converting a particularly barbarous African tribe. As the story develops, we discover that not only is he physically removed from his native environment, but more significantly he is an exile from the true meaning of the Christianity he professes to teach. His religion has never been more than a means for him to settle his account with his "pig of a father," his teachers, "the whole of lousy Europe." He longed for nothing more than the power his religion gave him.

I dreamed of absolute power, the kind that makes people kneel down, that forces the adversary to capitulate, converts him in short, and the blinder, the crueler he is, the more he's sure of himself, mired in his own convic-

[121]

tion, the more his consent establishes the royalty of whoever brought about his collapse. (39)

Stubborn, hardheaded, and impulsive, he undertakes a mission into a remote community where strange and horrid rites are practiced. After being subjected to periodic torture and final mutilation by the barbarous tribe dwelling in this dread-provoking city of salt, he becomes the convert. He transforms the blind allegiance he had for Christ into an equally intolerant worship of the savages' idol Ra. His single understanding of Christianity, his praise for the Lord, is totally transferred to an adoration of "the immortal soul of hatred" (57). In words of violent emotion he repudiates what he had been taught of the history of the church:

I had been misled, solely the reign of malice was devoid of defects, I had been misled, truth is square, heavy, thick, it does not admit distinctions, good is an idle dream, an intention constantly postponed and pursued with exhausting effort, a limit never reached, its reign is impossible. Only evil can reach its limits and reign absolutely, it must be served to establish its visible kingdom, then we shall see, but what does "then" mean, only evil is present, down with Europe, reason, honor, and the cross. (54)

In a demented adoration of the sadistic god he has been compelled to worship, he takes a gun and lies in ambush for another priest who has been sent to relieve him. He shoots the priest and is killed himself by the tribesmen who have followed him.

In this nightmarish monologue, told in a series of flashbacks, Camus is certainly experimenting with the stream-of-consciousness technique popularized in France by the writings of William Faulkner;[3] however, more significant than the stylistic experiment is the repetition here of one of the central themes of the entire collection of short stories. Camus is once again saying that man's inherent goodness can be so easily misdirected by chance. By a misunderstanding of meaning, by the chance of being born "bright but . . . pigheaded" (35), one can be totally misguided.

Because of reasons beyond his control, this missionary mistook his will to power for charity. He left the monastery convinced that he could convert the barbarous tribes to his religion. It is, of course, he who becomes the convert, and the overwhelming failure of his mission results in his imprisonment and the eventual transfer of the unthinking allegiance he had to Christ to a blind worship of the savages' idol. The insoluble conflict here results from the clash of two equally wrong commitments. Both the extremes of Christianity and of paganism are impossible for man to follow. In either case he becomes an exile from the kingdom of man. To underline the need for tolerance in order to live within the earthly realm, the true nature of tolerance and humility which he had always ignored is revealed to the missionary at the moment of his death: "Cast off that hate-ridden face, be good now, we were mistaken, we'll begin all over again, we'll rebuild the city of mercy, I want to go home" (61).

In some ways reminiscent of Cottard in *La Peste*, this young missionary too cannot know the kingdom of "fraternal man." The anguish, torture, and pain inflicted upon Cottard and the central figure here are caused by an ill-defined something that Camus again and again refuses to make explicit, but one which is nonetheless a powerful negative aspect of his universe. It is the theme of misunderstanding certainly, and here it is directed to two forces within rather than outside of man. Without reading too much into the character of Jean-Baptiste Clamence, it is a restatement of this same thesis. Good and evil are equally inherent in man, and it is a question of chance as to which will dominate.

VI   *"Les Muets"*

On a less individual level and certainly on a more melancholy and personal one, "Les Muets" is again a statement of the theme of misunderstanding and lack of communication among men. This story, unlike the first two, does not only involve the relationship of one individual to his universe; but in a very realistic, simple, and direct way, it also presents the complex problem of man out of tune with his fellow man and his times.

On an impersonal level, "Les Muets" is a story of the inevitable changes brought about by an evolving economy. These men, returning to work after twenty days of unsuccessful striking, are helplessly caught between two equally right forces. Cooperage, their trade, was threatened by the building of tankers and tank trucks and simply was not thriving. On the one hand, the cooper could not change his trade, "you don't change trades when you've gone to the trouble of learning one"; while on the other hand, the only way the employer could maintain a necessary margin of profit was to block wages. Characteristic of most of the conflicts which Camus presents, there is no obvious solution to the dilemma. Neither the men nor the boss is either totally right or totally wrong. The men were forced to return to work because of "wives sad at home" (67) or their own discouragement, but they resented the fact that their mouths had been closed; and the anger and helplessness hurt so much that they could not even cry out in protest. "They were men, after all" (78). Out of frustration and in order to give some expression to their dissatisfaction, they formed a coalition of silence against their employer's plea to "try to work together" (76).

But the story is not only concerned with the obviously immense complexities involved in a changing society. It is further complicated by the personal and human problems of the individual men. "Les Muets" is also a story about the loss of youth, the loss of the physical happiness of "the deep, clear water, the hot sun, the girls" (64). In the same way that inevitable progress had outdated the craftsmanship of the cooper, the natural progress of time had stolen from him "the habit of those violent days that used to satiate him" (64). Now, at forty, he is out of harmony not only with his times but also with time. Forced into a position that offers little promise of financial betterment, he is also void of any youthful hope of escape "across the sea."

It is a human predicament that Camus presents here—a problem particularly intense in his native Algeria—and he presents it with compassion and sympathetic understanding. The kingdom that all of these men long for is the realm of love and understanding, and the exile that they suffer is their exclusion from the fraternal universe. The only unity that they eventually find is the unity of all men in family affection, but even here they are incapable of communication and remain silent. Yet, optimistically, Camus implies that in the unspoken solidarity that the men experience through their reactions to the illness of their employer's daughter; in their own renewed contact with the twilight beauty of the earth and sea around them; and in their love for their own wives and families, they are at least momentarily reintegrated into the kingdom of man.

It is clear from the first three stories of the collection that most of Camus' characters suffer from the anxiety of having to decide their relationship to themselves and to others. If the examples that Camus uses seem marginal to ordinary human experience and at times inexplicable, it must be remembered that these stories continue his exploration of the difficulties that beset the exile in his lonely and independent efforts to be a man—an attempt that is, as Tarrou said in *La Peste*, more ambitious than to be a saint. And it must also be remembered that the absurd truth of life is that only in man's exile can he see the faint glimmerings of his kingdom.

The Kingdom of Man

VII *"L'Hôte"*

In "L'Hôte," a story of tragic misunderstanding, a schoolteacher in North Africa is given the task of delivering to the authorities an Arab accused of killing his cousin in a quarrel over grain. By every means available to him, Daru, the teacher, attempts to give the Arab his freedom. Although he cannot speak the Arab's language, he conveys his understanding of and sympathy for him by feeding and looking after him. He refuses to bind him and is disappointed when he does not attempt to escape during the night. The next morning Daru takes his charge to a point where two paths lead in divergent directions. Turning him toward the road which leads to the desert and to freedom, and away from the road which leads toward the town, toward judgment and prison, Daru leaves the Arab to make his own decision. As Daru returns toward the schoolhouse, he looks back and sees the Arab "slowly walking along the road to prison" (109).

When the schoolmaster returns to his classroom, he finds written in clumsily chalked-up words, "You handed over our brother. You will pay for this" (109). This threat by an invisible witness and the complete misunderstanding of his intended generosity make Daru painfully aware that "In this vast landscape he had loved so much, he was alone" (109).

Daru's helplessness and frustration, resulting from his inability to communicate the true meaning of his actions to the Arab, poignantly illustrate the position of the modern man who refrains from accepting the dogmatic pronouncements of either political parties or systematic ideologies. Daru is unable to ally himself with either the French administration or the Arab rebel movement. The only thing that he can be certain of is that the "rotten spite . . . tireless hates . . . blood lusts" (93) of man against man have solved nothing in the past and are unlikely to better the social, economic, and political conditions of the future. Although Daru's actions result in the seemingly negative and meaningless facts that he offended the gendarme, that the Arab chose punishment over freedom, that he himself is now exposed to an unjustifiable reprisal, he has maintained his dignity as a man who believes that "it's worth more to be wrong without killing anyone and in allowing others to talk, than to be right in the midst of silence and charnel houses" (*Actuelles* I, 267).

There is no easy solution for the characters caught in Camus' paradox of exile and kingdom. In "Les Muets" and "L'Hôte," he depicts men's failure to communicate as one half of the paradox;

and in "Jonas, ou l'Artiste au Travail," he completes the paradox by allowing Jonas to destroy his own integrity through his futile attempts to enter the lives of everyone he knows. It is not until the last story of the collection that the paradox between exile and kingdom is resolved into a final synthesis, a temporary conquering of separation and isolation.

VIII *"Jonas"*

"Jonas," in spite of its underlying serious meaning, is the wittiest and most amusing of Camus' writings. The story involves a Parisian painter of modest talent who rightfully trusted in his "star" to bring him fame and good fortune. After he was discovered by an art dealer, he was immediately beset by fame and its consequent frustrations. As he became better known, new friends arrived in scores to invade his already crowded apartment and to while away his afternoons "begging Jonas to go on working . . . for they . . . knew the value of an artist's time" (125). It soon became increasingly impossible for Jonas to paint at all. He was constantly surrounded by disciples who "explained to him at length what he had painted and why," and in this way "Jonas discovered in his work many intentions that rather surprised him, and a host of things he hadn't put there" (127).

Gradually Jonas completely lost his natural approach to his art and assumed the pose expected of him by his admirers. As time passed he painted less and less, but ironically enough, "the less he worked, the more his reputation grew" (131). The more his name appeared in print, the more often he was asked to take part "in exposing most revolting injustices" (133). The more his apartment was invaded by people who had respect for him but did not know or care about his work, the less he was the artist they professed to praise. Amidst the confusion caused by the visitors, disciples, and critics jammed into a flat that was already too small for his wife and three children, Jonas finally was totally absorbed into activities other than creative. His inspiration left him at the height of his fame. When he was asked to pose for a portrait of the artist at work, he himself no longer had either the time or the spirit to paint.

Frantically searching for somewhere peaceful to paint, Jonas, in a series of bizarre moves, abandoned his studio for the bedroom, the bedroom for the corridor, the corridor for the shower room, the shower room for the kitchen. But his star began to fail him, and now no matter where he was "he would think of painting, of his vocation, instead of painting" (144). In desperation he turned to cognac and women and was temporarily consoled with the illusion of creativity and vitality. At times it even seemed to him that his old strength was returning; and one day, encouraged by one of his female friends, he returned home to begin again. He constructed a kind of loft in a high corner of his flat and retreated there to meditate and "discover what he had not yet clearly understood although he had always known it and had always painted as if he knew it. He had to grasp at last that secret which was not merely the secret of art, as he could now see" (153). After many days of retreat, during which he saw only his friend Radeau and ate practically nothing, he fell ill. Radeau took the canvas on which Jonas had been working and found written "in very small letters a word that could be made out, but without any certainty as to whether it should be read *solitary* or *solidary*" (158).

Based upon Camus' personal experiences, and beyond its satirical and humorous aspects, the story is intended to reflect Camus' concern about the role of the artist in society. In his notebooks and in many of his essays and lectures, he frequently endeavored to come to some sort of understanding of his own commitment to art. In an interview with Jean Bloch-Michel, Camus underscored the position of the contemporary writer who is forced to choose between total engagement or total isolation:

That's how it is with the artist of our age: he runs the risk, if he stays in his ivory tower, of cutting himself off from reality, or, if he gallops forever around the political arena, of drying up. The ticklish paths of true art lie somewhere between the two. It seems to me that the writer should not ignore the conflicts of his time, and that he should take part in them when he knows that he can. But he should also keep, or from time to time recover, a definite perspective towards our history. Every work presupposes some factual content to which a creator has given shape. Though the artist should share in the misfortunes of his age, he must also try to stand off a bit to contemplate and formalize what he sees. This eternal return, this tension which can be, frankly, a dangerous game at times, is the burden of the artist today. Perhaps this means that, in short order, there will no longer be any artists. But maybe not. It is a question of time, of energy, of freedom, and also of chance.[4]

I have quoted the above passage at length, for it clearly and best expresses Camus' own conviction that it is impossible to dictate to an artist that he must live surrounded by the same preoccupations as the ordinary man; and this idea is the same one that is central in the story of Jonas. According to Camus, the artist is most atuned to his times when he is most solitary, and only by granting him this right can he find the necessary energy to create great art and through his creation make "the human visage more admirable and richer."

IX "La Pierre qui pousse"

It is not to the artist, but to life as an art that Camus turns in the final story of *L'Exil et le Royaume*. In many ways "La Pierre qui pousse" is not only the most compelling story of the collection, but it also presents a dramatic statement of and an at least temporary solution to many of the problems that have run through Camus' work from the time of his first essays. In all of his writings—never negating his original premise that God does not exist—he continually searched for a kind of victory over the absurdity of man's condition. Sometimes he judged and criticized what he found in the world about him; sometimes he turned to his own actions and passions as the material for his analysis; but the fundamental question that runs throughout all of his work remained the same. He consistently and directly asked for a clear and concise definition of what it meant to be a man.

"La Pierre qui pousse" gives one possible answer to this question. It tells of a French engineer who has left his native Europe in order to build a dam in the small Brazilian town of Iguape. His arrival at the village coincides with an annual religious festival. The natives look upon D'Arrast, the engineer, as an outsider; and he is, in fact, an outsider in many ways. He not only comes from another continent with a contrasting culture; but he also is a Catholic who, according to his own admission, never found his "place" within the church. Perhaps even more striking than these facts is that his self-inflicted exile from a Europe with "shame and wrath" is emphasized by his questionable passport and by his attempted escape from his past guilt. He tells the cook, "Someone was about to die through my fault" (187).

In this remote village, D'Arrast continues to find it difficult to enter into any sort of real contact with other men, until, on the day before the festival, a village cook tells him of a vow he made years before when he was in imminent danger of drowning. "So I told the good Jesus," he says, "that at his procession I would carry a hundred-pound stone on my head if he saved me. You don't have to believe me, but the waters became calm and my heart too. I swam slowly,

I was happy, and I reached the shore. Tomorrow I'll keep my promise" (183). Without really knowing why, other than for the simple reason that "he looked at the handsome frank face smiling trustingly at him, its dark skin gleaming with health and vitality" (185), D'Arrast promises to help the cook keep his pledge. This is D'Arrast's first step toward actual communication with the villagers. That evening there is a celebration in honor of St. George. D'Arrast observes the natives' frenzied singing and dancing, becomes entranced by the violent beating of the drums, the heat, the dust, the smoke, and the smell of bodies; but he remains an outsider and is unable to forget himself totally and join the natives' sacrifice of their own individuality. He is brutally reminded of the fact that he is an alien when the cook tells him, "They are going to dance all night long, but they don't want you to stay now" (197).

He does not enter into an emotionally satisfying contact with these people until the day of the holy procession. As in the past, the cook takes up his burden and joins the procession, but it soon becomes evident that his strength is not equal to the heavy task. He falters, sweats and strains, and finally collapses in an agony of body and spirit. D'Arrast leaps to his side, lifts the stone to his own head, and proceeds toward the church. He had already gone beyond the center of the church square when "without knowing why, he veered off to the left and turned away from the church" (210). He reaches the cook's hovel, his breath beginning to fail, his arms trombling under the stone; and brusquely hurled the stone onto the still glowing fire in the center of the room" (212). There "he felt rising within him a surge of obscure and panting joy that he was powerless to name" (212). He acclaims once again "a fresh beginning in life." Through his actions, D'Arrast has declared his brotherhood with all men who labor and are heavy laden. That his actions are understood is made clear by the natives' invitation to "Sit down with us" (213). No longer a stranger, D'Arrast has conquered his separation and loneliness and has found a place where he belongs.

It is characteristic of Camus' point of view that in this story he transferred the shrine from the church to the hearth of a man who has the courage to keep a promise freely made. Never conceiving himself to be an abstract philosopher, Camus' consistent concern has been to communicate an individual experience that is illuminated and universalized through his art. Rather than depending on abstractions to convey his ideas, the impact of his total work depends heavily on the frequently unresolved tensions that he presents in his narratives. D'Arrast in this final story has found his place in the community of Iguape, but there is no implied guarantee that his happiness will endure. It matters little if it does not. The important thing is that he has found meaning to his life through his complete involvement in human experience and action.

X *Evaluation*

In many ways, this collection of short stories is both a beginning and an end. As I have said earlier, Camus—for the moment at least—was willing to turn away from abstract philosophy and to concentrate upon human beings in actual situations. Many critics have pointed out that these stories were partially experiments in style for a projected novel, "Le Premier homme." And as the reader moves from one story to the next, he cannot doubt that the collection is an almost virtuoso display of technical variety. Camus proves over and over again that his power to evoke place and atmosphere is as great as his ability to show man in his duality of body and spirit. Not only do his people live and breathe, but the features of the scenes surrounding them stand out with an arresting clarity.

Yet, as is always true in Camus' writing, the value of the graphic and descriptive passages is to highlight the central theme of the book: the exile and the kingdom of man. One might say that this is but another facet of Camus' never-ending exploration of the difficulties that beset the exile in his lonely efforts to understand the universe, to understand and be understood by his fellow man. From the earliest writings to these last stories, Camus has consistently attempted to understand the evils and weaknesses within man and within the world in order to realize that the only possible kingdom attainable to man is not a kingdom of heaven for the submissive, but a kingdom of humanity attainable through free and energetic assumption of individual responsibility.

His plea for man to accept the human condition and through courage surpass his limitations is heard most clearly in *L'Exil et le Royaume*. The deeper he looks into life and the more agonizing his perception of its inconsistencies becomes, his reaction is not to despair but to find more courage and faith in his own ability to become a decent human being, to keep from crumbling under the darkness of his vision of humanity.

CHAPTER 10

Conclusion

I *Camus' Position in Twentieth-Century Letters*

LATE in the 1960's, more than eight years since Camus' fatal accident, it is still very difficult to predict the exact position he will occupy in twentieth-century literature. Today when we speak of our century we must project one-third of its allotted time into the future. In the vast history of civilization, thirty-three years is perhaps infinitesimal, but one need pause but a moment to realize that it is sufficient time for a second Shakespeare to baffle mankind with the beauties of his verse; time too for an unknown Columbus to discover a whole new world somewhere in unexplored space; or for a scholar to find the unpublished manuscripts of a Blake or a Kierkegaard. The hectic rapidity of the changes in every aspect of civilized living has made even the least percipient of us hesitant to judge anything today without knowing tomorrow. The unknown of the future can be an extremely potent force.

There is a second reason that also makes its difficult to categorize dogmatically Camus' future reputation. Without fully trusting the timeworn truism that greater objectivity can be obtained when a writer's work is removed to some temporal distance from the critic, I find myself calling upon that truism in this particular situation. One has only to think of Heidegger, Whitehead, Jung, St. John Perse, Faulkner, Dürrenmatt, Thomas Mann, Rilke, Tennessee Williams, André Malraux, Graham Greene, Bernanos, Robert Frost, T. S. Eliot, Martin Buber, Karl Jaspers, Sartre, Kafka, Proust, Henry Miller, Hemingway—to name twenty-one outstanding poets, novelists, philosophers, and playwrights of the past sixty years, and his immediate response to such a random list is not one of amazement over the unquestionable greatness of these men, but it is rather one of amazement over the fact that he has omitted such established people as Gide, Toynbee, Tillich, Mauriac, Brecht, etc., etc., etc. It becomes a kind of literary game to pick and choose the favorite players of the moment. Can any one of us with complete objective assurance say that Camus is greater than Faulkner but less great than Mann, or Mann greater than Faulkner but not so great as Camus? I think that the absurdity of the game is immediately apparent.

So the task of placing Camus in his exact position is not an easy one. There is no doubt that his writings fit into the mainstream of twentieth-century thought. He, like many of the other writers mentioned, reflects the problematic existence that man in the Western world has been forced to endure following the calamities of the past fifty years. He, again as do most of these artists, tries to come to terms with himself and his world and to discover new values that will take the place of traditional theological and humanistic ones. What he creates to substitute for a belief in God or a belief in social and scientific progress also is not totally his, born full-blown from the head of Zeus. His literary and philosophical indebtedness is wide-reaching, and he reflects the influence of his exposure to the Greek classics, to the writings of his fellow countrymen such as Madame de Lafayette, Gide, Proust, Malraux, and Montherlant, to the German Kafka, the Russians Dostoevski and Tolstoy, to the theatrical masterpieces of Molière, Shakespeare, Lope de Vega, to the Americans Melville, Hemingway, and Faulkner. This impressive list does not actually distinguish Camus from many writers of our century—as a matter of fact, the list itself hardly distinguishes him from any well-educated person today. But the thought and art that he sought to emulate from these men does bear his particular stamp. These authors stimulated his mind and encouraged him to develop that quality—his uniqueness—which does set him apart from all of the writers of this time.

II Camus' Intellectual Odyssey

In Camus' wrestling with man's condition, as we proceed from one work to the other, there is ever present a strong voice that is speaking for itself, in humility and trust, to an audience that has undergone experiences parallel to his own. The strength of his voice tells his audience that it need not suffer alone. Although the world may remain somewhat incomprehensible, though events may happen that are inexplicable; yet he tells us that we are free to search for a unifying principle in our lives, that if we do inquire into the problems of existence, we can derive something out of life other than eating, drinking, sleeping, dressing, and undressing.

Conclusion

It is Camus' insistence that we constantly reach upward—not to an unknown Heaven—but to a better understanding of the present moment that provides his unique contribution to modern thought. His allegiance to the values of man, of moderation, and of nature gives a positive character to his writing and distinguishes it from much of contemporary writing which offers man nothing other than negative awareness. He tells us that the world is absurd, but that there are reasons to want to go on living; and it is from this desire to live that we can begin to build and create a universe closer to what we would like it to be. It is the image of Sisyphus that comes to mind here; and although it may be difficult to imagine Sisyphus happy, it is not impossible to grant Sisyphus' triumph over despair. Camus finds meaning in Sisyphus' and in man's struggle to create meaning in an absurd world, and it is this faint glimmer of hope that he holds before us that makes his voice stronger than many at this particular time.

He is a man of his age. His writings not only reflect the conflicts, the violence, the lack of communication that are a part of our everyday world, but they also reveal his private concern with the far-reaching problems of this century. As we follow his intellectual odyssey from the recognition of absurdity through his complex development of revolt, we are made increasingly aware of the conflicting demands of modern life. What we may have subconsciously perceived as the reasons for our instability are made unquestionably clear through his projection of our own frustrations into the central characters of his imaginative writings. There is no doubt that these heroes reflect the spirit and the pulse of contemporary life. Like them we tend to live from day to day with little sense of an enduring purpose and meaning in life, and also like them we try to work out for ourselves a satisfying philosophy to give life some direction and purpose. They, as we, have inherited the uncertainties of our age. It is no longer possible to assume the moral and religious convictions which our ancestors took for granted. The ultimate meaning that they found in religious or humanistic terms has been weakened—if not totally shattered—by the disturbing facts of the past fifty years. The poet Auden said that "Aloneness is man's real condition," and Camus echoes his voice; but unlike most voices of this century, Camus is not willing to stop there. Once he subscribes to man's aloneness, he sets out to create new values that will again give life meaning and man a responsible role in the universe.

It is through his art that Camus explores an experience which gives an exact image of man within the intellectual climate of the twentieth century. He endows his characters with attitudes, feelings, and experiences latent among all men; and through his characters he makes us aware of the anxieties, the isolation, and the anonymity of man in contemporary society. He forces us to realize that scientific and technological advancement, and the consequent material comforts, actually have nothing to do with happiness. He leads us to the painful discovery that rather than progressing, we are in the midst of the greatest decline ever experienced by any civilization. Instead of feeling more at home in the world through the conquests of science, we find ourselves alone and frightened in an indifferent universe. He diagnoses the characteristics of our age and relives in art the fundamental problems of life common to all of us. What emerges is not only a communication of personal experience, but also a valid work of art concerned with concrete problems in today's world.

As Camus leads his reader from *L'Envers et l'endroit* to *L'Exil et le Royaume,* he gradually evolves a philosophy that bears his particular seal. From the cosmic pessimism which characterized *Le Mythe de Sisyphe* to the philosophy of revolt most clearly developed in *L'Homme révolté,* he constantly corrects, without ever completely negating, his original position. He begins his absurd experiment with *L'Étranger* and *Le Mythe de Sisyphe.* In their denunciation of hope and their refusal of any metaphysical comfort for man, these books artistically reflect Camus' provisional attitude toward the contradiction between man's longing for immortality and the inevitability of his death. As we have seen, his aim from the beginning was only to examine and not to proffer the philosophy of the absurd. From his search for truth in a world that offers no hope and no illusions, he found that man was left with the right to challenge the world at every moment, to be passionately aware of every experience, and to be conscious of his freedom to exhaust everything that is given.

The next step in Camus' experiment was to test these concepts in order to discover whether or not human dignity could persist in a world that granted each individual unlimited freedom. In the characterization of Meursault, Camus had already implied that man could not live happily or productively if all events were thought to be equal, but it is in the dramas of *Le Malentendu* and *Caligula* that the specific idea of freedom is pushed to its limits. The mad Emperor Caligula's attempt to transform the world by exercising his unbounded freedom is more spectacular than that of Jan in *Le Malentendu,* but both men are defeated by a very simple truth that they failed to recognize. There is a standard of values inherent in human nature which, as Cherea says, finds certain actions "more beautiful than others." At this juncture in the development of his thought, Camus imposes a limit upon human freedom. All actions are not equivalent and a judgment of them can be made without invoking sources beyond human experience. He is increasingly aware of the relationship between individual happiness and the attitude and conduct of others; and he clearly sees that a world void of a belief in moral principles, in which the individual is free to act in accordance with his own desires, could lead to a total disregard for the life and the welfare of others. He now adds to the original concept of absurdity the idea of limits. Man is no longer completely free.

In our discussion of Camus' early writings, we mentioned that the idea of limits was implicit in *L'Etranger* and clearly stated in *Caligula.* At this early date Camus was aware that the absurdity of the world was a fact that had to be accepted, but he was equally aware of another fact. He realized that although the world could not be altered, man who suffers from its absurdity could. The implication of man's ability to create a life of his own that has meaning, unity, and value runs throughout all of Camus' writing, but it is only clearly defined in the works following *Caligula.* No one can doubt that it is the philosophy of revolt which dominates his thinking from that time until his death. He abandons the futile problem of death in an absurd world and focuses upon the problem of life. He accepts the world as it is but he is not willing to accept man as he is. Man may never be able to defeat the injustice of the universe, but he can defeat the injustice of his fellow man. The world is absurd because that is the nature of the universe, but history need not be absurd, for it is controlled by man. The oppression which man suffers because of false ideas and ideologies can be eliminated, and it is to the specific condemnation of human error that Camus turns his attention after *Caligula.* His rebellion is directed against those men and institutions that refuse to respect the value of human nature and to accept the clearly defined limits of human behavior.

It is with *La Peste* that Camus switches his emphasis from the intellectual problems of the universe to the more personal problems of individual man. Here he investigates the possibility of finding a series of values not only to satisfy the individual man but also to be commended to others on universal grounds. He finds these values in the basic dignity of man and the inherent value of each individual human life. Camus himself remarked that *La Peste* indicated a change from "an attitude of solitary revolt to the recognition of a community whose struggles all must share." And in the same way that the absurd experiment was carried to its extreme in the two earlier dramas, *Le Malentendu* and *Caligula,* the idea of revolt and limits is now further analyzed in *L'Etat de Siège* and *Les Justes.* It is in these plays that he searches for the humanitarian spirit which again restores the value of an individual human life. Man is now placed in the enviable position of being able to realize high human ideals through the exercise of his own moral consciousness.

If we think back to the theory expressed in *Le Mythe de Sisyphe* and contrast it to the ideas expressed in *L'Homme révolté,* the distance which separates the literature of the absurd from the literature of revolt becomes increasingly clear. In *Le Mythe de Sisyphe,* Camus stated that "For the absurd man, it is no longer a question of explaining or resolving, but of feeling and describing. All begins with a clear-visioned indifference. To describe: this is the ultimate ambition of absurd thinking" (131). By contrast, in the literature of revolt, man can no longer afford to be an indifferent stranger. He lives in the same absurd world, bereft of all metaphysical aid; but rather than being satisfied to describe that world, Camus now insists that man must fashion a world of unity and value. He realized that in a completely absurd world the only values that could be established would be created from an extremely personal point of view and would only be tenable in a particular historical epoch. The solitary reflections of a Sisyphus must therefore give way to the forceful actions of a Prometheus. Through his own "sweat and blood" man must conquer his values and formulate an attitude which will do justice to the human condition. There is no room for apathy and resignation. Man must act and through his actions establish an order that carries him beyond negation to the affirmation of life.

It is at this point that the experiment should be concluded. The original premise has been investigated by the essayist and clarified by the novelist and playwright. The individual has grappled with the forces that menace his freedom, and, by the strength of his own intelligence and sympathy, he has emerged victorious. Through an intense and honest inquiry into the nature of man and the universe, Camus has molded a formless mass into a coherent whole. The world may still deny man his rightful place, but the conscious man can regain his lost kingdom by constantly using his intelligence to oppose, control, and destroy the social patterns which oppress him. The experiment should have ended, but it did not.

Not satisfied with the image of man that he had discovered through his investigation of the absurd and of the philosophy of revolt, Camus now begins his analysis of the other side of the coin. His portrayal of Clamence in *La Chute* as a man who not only knows himself to be self-centered, dishonest, and hypocritical but as one who also seeks to prove to other men that they are exactly like him, injects a measure of pessimism into Camus' portrait of man that is almost completely foreign to his previous writings. Up to this time in the experiment, Camus insisted upon the innocence of man. Guilt was always an outside force found either in the natural injustice of the world or in the evil of false ideas. In *La Chute*, Clamence leads us to believe that man's suffering is more self-imposed than it is caused by any external factor. This almost totally pessimistic portrayal of man as a creature of both good and evil, whose bad faith can destroy even his best intentions, seemingly introduces an entirely new concept into Camus' thought. But it too can be seen as an extension rather than a negation of his earlier ideas. The problem posed here is an intensely personal one. Given the universe of *L'Etranger*, the society of *La Peste*, the question now turns inward and asks what man can accomplish in the attempt to control the evil of an individual human conscience.

La Chute, then, may be the beginning of a new phase of Camus' experiment with life, or it could be a dramatic conclusion. In some ways Camus has led us through the complete cycle of self-evaluation. Given the freedom that is granted by the absurdity of the world, if this freedom is not controlled and corrected by an ever-questioning conscience, it has the dangerous potential of leading man into the abyss of self-negation and the negation of the world he lives in. In a world that demands the active engagement of every aware man, the acute introspection of a Clamence could lead to total inactivity and the destruction of all that is good in man.

But whether *La Chute* is a beginning or an end becomes an academic question of little consequence. The truth is that we will never know. As Sartre remarked, Camus' early death has forced us to look upon an incomplete body of work as his final testimony. It is futile to romanticize about what might have been, what "Le Premier homme" could have said. The brutal fact is that there is no future promise. Perhaps that is what Camus was saying all along:

the tomorrows that might have been have little or nothing to do with the today that is. And it is "the today" that is Camus' passionate concern.

His completed work stands as a testimony to a man who was profoundly concerned with his times. His thought progresses from a personal involvement with the universe to an understanding of it that is acceptable on human terms. It is the human element that consistently enters into Camus' thought and prohibits a strictly systematic approach to any individual piece of his writing. We have said that Camus thinks aloud through his writings, and just as thought is a constantly evolving process, so too is his experimental philosophizing. His philosophy never attains completion, but like Clamence, Camus recognizes that he lives in a time when there can never be a completion. The best that man can do is to remain faithful to those things that he knows to be true. Those few things that Camus has illuminated for our times have broadened our range of sympathies and our consciousness of what goes on around us. He has made us see and appreciate "the beautiful face of the world" and taste the richness of life. Life is more interesting and more worth the living than it would have seemed without his work. Like the great artists before him, he has helped to create the myths by which we live.

Notes and References

Wherever possible, I have cited editions of Camus' works which are readily accessible to American students.

Preface

1. *Noces* (Paris, 1947), p. 36. All succeeding page references are to this edition.

2. The purpose of this book is to give the uninitiated reader an idea of the evolution of Camus' art and thought. In no way does the book pretend to analyze every aspect of this development. For example, I have chosen not to discuss the various dramatic adaptations that Camus made nor do I discuss his journalistic writings in depth. These aspects of his work have been thoroughly studied in other critical essays and did not seem to warrant repetition here.

Chapter 1

1. "Create Dangerously," *Resistance, Rebellion and Death,* trans. Justin O'Brien (New York, 1961), p. 266.

2. For a detailed presentation and a clear analysis of Camus' journalistic writings, see Emmett Parker, *Albert Camus: The Artist in the Arena* (Madison, 1965).

3. Personal letter, dated Paris, le 3 déc. 1951. L'histoire du MALENTENDU a été lu réellement dans un journal. Je l'ai introduit dans L'ETRANGER parce j'avais l'intention, en effet, d'en faire une pièce. De meme que vous avez remarqué à juste titre qu'il est ques-tion de L'ETRANGER dans LA PESTE. Il s'agit là, non d'une petite mystification, mais une manière d'indiquer à de très rares lecteurs attentifs que, dans mon esprit au moins, mes livres ne doivent pas être jugés un à un, mais dans leur ensemble et dans leur déroulement.

4. *The Myth of Sisyphus,* trans. Justin O'Brien (New York, 1955), p. 18. All succeeding page references are to this edition.

5. I am indebted to Germaine Brée's, John Cruickshank's, and Philip Thody's studies on Camus for most of the biographical information contained in this book.

6. *Essais* (Paris, 1965), pp. 1157–61.

Chapter 3

1. Much of the discussion of *L' Etranger* is based upon my earlier book, *The Urge to Live* (Chapel Hill, 1964).

2. *The Stranger,* trans. Stuart Gilbert (New York, 1959). All succeeding page references are to this edition.

3. *Caligula and Three Other Plays,* trans. Stuart Gilbert (New York, 1958). All succeeding page references are to this collection.

Chapter 4

1. "Sur l'avenir de la tragedie," *Théâtre, Récits, Nouvelles* (Paris, 1962), pp. 1699–1709.

2. The factual information pertaining to the production of Camus' play is taken from John Cruickshank, *Albert*

Camus and the Literature of Revolt (New York, 1960).

3. Trans. by Stuart Gilbert as *The Misunderstanding* in *Caligula and Three Other Plays*. All succeeding page references are to this collection.

Chapter 5

1. *The Plague*, trans. Stuart Gilbert (New York, 1948). All succeeding page references are to this edition.

2. Camus calls *La Peste* a "chronique" to distinguish it from a "roman" or "novel" in the usual sense of the word. The objective narration of the chronicle not only prevents the reader from total identification with the characters and the situation, but it also makes him more receptive to the symbolic implications of the work.

3. This is but one of the many possible interpretations. For example, many critics see *La Peste* as a symbolic presentation of the Nazi occupation of Paris during World War II.

4. Camus writes:
Yes, if it is a fact that people like to have examples given them, men of the type they call heroic, and if it is absolutely necessary that this narrative should include a 'hero,' the narrator commends to his readers, with, to his thinking, perfect justice, this insignificant and obscure hero who had to his credit only a little goodness of heart and a seemingly absurd ideal. This will render to the truth its due, to the addition of two and two its sum of four, and to heroism the secondary place that rightly falls to it, just after, never before, the noble claim of happiness. It will also give this chronicle its character, which is intended to be that of a narrative made with good feelings — that is to say, feelings that are neither demonstrably bad nor overcharged with emotion in the ugly manner of a stage-play. (126)

5. Cruickshank, p. 178.

6. See Emmett Parker's *Albert*

Camus for a thorough discussion of Camus' editorial writing.

Chapter 6

1. *Actuelles I, Chroniques 1944–1948* (Paris, 1950).

2. Preface to *Caligula and Three Other Plays*.

3. Trans. by Stuart Gilbert as *State of Siege* in *Caligula and Three Other Plays*. All succeeding page references are to this collection.

4. Trans. by Stuart Gilbert as *The Just Assassins* in *Caligula and Three Other Plays*. All succeeding page references are to this collection.

5. *The Rebel*, trans. Anthony Bower (New York, 1958). All succeeding page references are to this edition.

Chapter 7

1. Philip Thody, *Albert Camus, 1913–1960* (London, 1961), pp. 139–40.

2. Hermann Hesse, *Steppenwolf*, trans. Joseph Mileck and Horst Frenz (New York, 1963).

3. Thody, *loc. cit.*

4. Thody, p. 147.

5. Thody, p. 148.

6. Nicola Chiaromonte, "Sartre versus Camus: A Political Quarrel," *Camus*, ed. Germaine Brée (Englewood Cliffs, N. J., 1963), p. 35.

7. Chiaromonte, p. 34.

8. Cruickshank, p. 126.

9. See John Cruickshank's and Emmett Parker's studies on Camus for a thorough discussion of the Camus-Sartre debate.

10. Jean-Paul Sartre, "Tribute to Albert Camus," *Camus*, ed. Germaine Brée, p. 174.

Chapter 8

1. Preface to *La Ballade de lo géôle de Reading* by Oscar Wilde (Paris, 1952).

2. *Resistance, Rebellion and Death*, p. 266.

Notes and References

3. *The Fall,* trans. Justin O'Brien (New York, 1957). All succeeding page references are to this edition.

Chapter 9

1. *The Rebel,* p. 226.
2. *The Exile and the Kingdom,* trans. Justin O'Brien (New York, 1958). All succeeding page references are to this edition.

3. Camus was working on an adaptation of Faulkner's *Requiem for a Nun* at this time.

4. Albert Maquet, *Albert Camus: The Invincible Summer,* trans. Herma Briffault (New York, 1958), pp. 196–97.

Selected Bibliography

For the student interested in a complete collection of Camus' writings, the Pléiade editions of his works are indispensable. Volume I contains an extensive chronology of the major events in Camus' life; Volume II contains an equally extensive list of his writings. The student will also find the bibliographies in John Cruickshank's, Emmett Parker's, and Philip Thody's studies especially helpful.

The following list of Camus' writings is meant to provide a selected bibliography of his published works.

PRIMARY SOURCES

A. *Collected Writings*

1. *Théâtre, récits, nouvelles,* ed. ROGER QUILLIOT. ("Bibliothèque de la Pléiade.") Paris: Gallimard, 1962.

2. *Essais,* ed. ROGER QUILLIOT. ("Bibliothèque de la Pléiade.") Paris: Gallimard, 1965.

3. *Carnets: Mai 1935–février 1942.* Paris: Gallimard, 1962. Translated into English by PHILIP THODY, New York: Knopf, 1963.

4. *Carnets II: Janvier 1942–mars 1951.* Paris: Gallimard, 1964. Translated into English by PHILIP THODY, New York: Knopf, 1965.

B. *Major Works*

1. *L'Envers et l'endroit.* Algier: Charlot, 1936. Republished with a preface, Paris: Gallimard, 1958.

2. *Noces.* Angiers: Charlot, 1938. Republished, Paris: Gallimard, 1947.

3. *L'Etranger.* Paris: Gallimard, 1942. Translated into English by STUART GILBERT, New York: Vintage Books, 1958.

4. *Le Mythe de Sisyphe.* Paris: Gallimard, 1943. Translated into English by JUSTIN O'BRIEN, New York: Knopf, 1955.

5. *Lettres à un ami allemand.* Paris: Gallimard, 1945 (the first two of the four letters were published in 1943 and 1944 respectively). Translated into English by JUSTIN O'BRIEN in the collection *Resistance, Rebellion and Death,* New York: Knopf, 1961.

6. *Le Malentendu* and *Caligula.* Written in 1942–43, and 1938 respectively. Published together in book form in 1945. Republished in revised versions in 1958 by Gallimard. Translated into English by STUART GILBERT, New York: Knopf, 1958.

7. *La Peste.* Paris: Gallimard, 1947. Translated into English by STUART GILBERT, New York: Knopf, 1948.

8. *L'Etat de Siège.* Paris: Gallimard, 1948. Translated into English by STUART GILBERT, New York: Knopf, 1958.

9. *Les Justes.* Paris: Gallimard, 1950. Translated into English by STUART GILBERT, New York: Knopf, 1958.

10. *Actuelles, I, II, III.* Paris: Gallimard, 1950, 1953, 1958. Partially translated into English by JUSTIN O'BRIEN in the collection *Resistaince, Rebellion and Death,* New York: Knopf, 1961.

11. *L'Homme révolté.* Paris: Gallimard, 1951. Translated into English by

ANTHONY BOWER, New York: Vintage Books, 1958.

12. *L'Eté.* Paris: Gallimard, 1954.

13. *La Chute.* Paris: Gallimard, 1956. Translated into English by JUSTIN O'BRIEN, New York: Knopf, 1957.

14. *L'Exil et le Royaume.* Paris: Gallimard, 1957. Translated into English by JUSTIN O'BRIEN, New York: Knopf, 1958.

C. *Adaptations and Translations*

1. THURBER, JAMES. *The Last Flower (La Dernière Fleur).* Traduit par ALBERT CAMUS, Paris: Gallimard, 1952.

2. LA BARCA, CALDERÓN DE. *La Devoción de la Cruz (La Devotion à la Croix).* Texte français d'ALBERT CAMUS, Paris: Gallimard, 1953.

3. LARIVEY, PIERRE DE. *Les Esprits.* Adaptation d'ALBERT CAMUS , Paris: Gallimard, 1953.

4. BUZZATI, DINO. *Un caso clinico (Un Cas intéressant).* Adaptation d'ALBERT CAMUS, Paris: L'Avante-scène, 1955.

5. FAULKNER, WILLIAM. *Requiem for a Nun (Requiem pour une nonne).* Adaptation d'ALBERT CAMUS, Paris: Gallimard, 1956.

6. VEGA, LOPE DE. *El Caballero de Olmedo (Le Chevalier d'Olmedo).* Texte français d'ALBERT CAMUS, Paris: Gallimard, 1957.

7. DOSTOEVSKI, FYODOR. *Les Possédés.* Pièce en trois parties adaptée du roman de Dostoevski par ALBERT CAMUS, Paris: Gallimard, 1959. Adaptation translated into English by JUSTIN O'BRIEN, New York, 1960.

D. *Prefaces*

1. CHAMFORT, NICOLAS SÉBASTIEN ROCH DE. *Maximes et anecdotes.* Monaco: Dac, 1944.

2. SALVET, ANDRÉ. *Le Combat silencieux.* Paris: Editions France-Empire, 1945.

3. CLAIRIN, PIERRE-EUGÈNE. *Dix Estampes originales.* Paris: Rombaldi, 1946.

4. CHAR, RENÉ. *Feuillets d'Hypnos.* Paris: Gallimard, 1946.

5. LEYNAUD, RENÉ. *Poésies posthumes.* Paris: Gallimard, 1947.

6. MÉRY, JACQUES. *Laissez-passer mon peuple.* Paris: Editions due Seuil, 1947.

7. HÉON-CANONNE, JEANNE. *Devant la Mort.* Paris: Siraudeau, 1951.

8. MAUROC, DANIEL. *Contre-amour.* Paris: Editions de Minuit, 1952.

9. WILDE, OSCAR. *La Ballade de la géôle de Reading.* Paris: Falaize, 1952.

10. GUILLOUX, LOUIS. *La Maison du peuple, suivi de Compagnons.* Paris: Grasset, 1953.

11. ROSMER, ALFRED. *Moscou sous Lenine: Les Origines du communisme.* Paris: Editions de Flore, 1953.

12. BIEBER, KONRAD. *L'Allemagne vue par les écrivains de la Résistance française.* Genève: Droz, 1954.

13. TARGUEBAYRE, CLAIRE. *Cordes-en-Albigeois.* Toulouse: Plon, 1954.

14. CAMUS, ALBERT. *L'Etranger,* eds. GERMAINE BRÉE and CARLOS LYNES, JR. New York: Appleton-Century-Crofts, 1955.

15. DU GARD, ROGER MARTIN. *Oeuvres complètes.* Paris: Gallimard, 1956.

16. FAULKNER, WILLIAM. *Requiem pour une nonne.* Paris: Gallimard, 1957.

17. *La Vérité sur l'affaire Nagy.* Paris: Plon, 1958.

18. GRENIER, JEAN. *Les Iles.* Paris: Gallimard, 1959.

E. *Works Written in Collaboration with Other Writers*

1. "L'Intelligence et l'échafaud," in J. PREVOST (ed.), *Problèmes du roman, Confluences,* special no. (July/August, 1943). Contains articles on the novel by Valéry, Arland, Prevost *et al.*

2. "Remarque sur la révolte," in

Selected Bibliography

JEAN GRENIER (ed.), *L'Existence*. Paris: Gallimard, 1945.

3. "Rencontres avec André Gide," in *Hommage à André Gide, Nouvelle Revue Française* (1951).

4. "Herman Melville," in RAYMOND QUENEAU (ed.), *Les Ecrivains célèbres*. Paris: Mazenod, 1953.

5. *Désert vivant: Images en couleurs de Walt Disney*. Textes de Marcel Aymé, Louis Bromfield, Albert Camus. Paris: Société française du livre, 1954.

6. ARTHUR KOESTLER and ALBERT CAMUS. *Réflexions sur la peine capitale*. Paris: Calmann-Levy, 1954.

SECONDARY SOURCES

For complete bibliographies of secondary source material, I refer the reader to D. W. ALDEN (general ed.), *Bibliography of Critical and Biographical References for the Study of Contemporary French Literature*, New York: Stechert-Hafner, 1949 onwards; RENATE BOLLINGER, *Albert Camus: Eine Bibliographie der Literatur über ihn und sein Werk*, Köln: Greyen Verlag, 1957; and SIMONE CREPIN, *Albert Camus: Essai de bibliographie*, Bruxelles: Commission Belge de Bibliographie, 1960.

With the exception of Jean-Claude Brisville's and Morvan Lebesque's books on Camus, I have included only those full-length studies done in English that I found particularly useful in the preparation of this book.

1. BRÉE, GERMAINE. *Camus*. New Brunswick: Rutgers University Press, 1961. An especially informative book which contains many interesting and relevant biographical facts. Germaine Brée had access to Camus' private notebooks while he was still alive and her use of this material gives her book a special biographical value.

2. ———— (ed.). *Camus: A Collection of Critical Essays*. Englewood Cliffs: Prentice-Hall, 1962. Written by outstanding critics, these essays give the reader some idea of the wide range of the critical writing done on Camus. The collection contains the famous "Explication of *The Stranger*" by Jean-Paul Sartre.

3. BRISVILLE, JEAN-CLAUDE. *Camus*. Paris: Gallimard, 1959. Especially interesting for its iconography.

4. CRUICKSHANK, JOHN. *Albert Camus and the Literature of Revolt*. New York: Oxford University Press, 1960. Most comprehensive of all studies on Camus, contains an excellent literary and philosophical analysis of Camus' works.

5. HANNA, THOMAS. *The Thought and Art of Albert Camus*. Chicago: Henry Regnery Co., 1958. The evolution of Camus' art and thought is carefully and clearly studied.

6. LEBESQUE, MORVAN. *Camus par lui-même*. Paris: Editions du Seuil, 1963. Like Brisville's book, also interesting for its iconography.

7. PARKER, EMMETT. *Albert Camus: The Artist in the Arena*. Madison: University of Wisconsin Press, 1965. Contains an outstanding analysis and a thorough bibliography of Camus' editorial writing.

8. RHEIN, PHILLIP H. *The Urge to Live*. Chapel Hill: University of North Carolina Press, 1964. Comparison of Camus' *L'Etranger* with Kafka's *Der Prozess*. Provides new insight into Camus' writing.

9. THODY, PHILIP. *Albert Camus: 1913–1960*. London: Hamish Hamilton, 1961. Clearly written, perceptive analysis of Camus' writings; thorough coverage of his critical reception in England, France, and the United States.

Of the hundreds of articles in print on the various aspects of Camus' writings, I have chosen a few of the better-known ones that have appeared in English. For more complete bibliographies, I again refer the reader to D. W.

Alden, Renate Bollinger, and Simone Crepin.

The titles of the following articles clearly indicate their content.

1. BRÉE, GERMAINE. "Albert Camus and *The Plague,*" *Yale French Studies,* 8 (1951), 93–100.

2. BROMBERT, VICTOR. "Camus and the Novel of the Absurd," *Yale French Studies,* 1 (1948), 119–23.

3. FROHOCK, WILBUR M. "Camus: Image, Influence, and Sensibility," *Yale French Studies,* 2 (1949), 91–99.

4. LANSER, KERMIT, "Albert Camus," *Kenyon Review,* XIV, 4 (1952), 562–78.

5. MOHRT, MICHEL. "Ethic and Poetry in the Work of Camus," *Yale French Studies,* 1 (1948), 113–18.

6. PEYRE, HENRI. "Camus: An Anti-Christian Moralist," *Proceedings of the American Philosophical Society,* CII, 5 (October, 1958), 477–82.

7. ROSSI, LOUIS. "Albert Camus: The Plague of Absurdity," *The Kenyon Review,* XX, 4 (Summer, 1958), 399–422.

8. ROUDIEZ, LEON S. "The Literary Climate of *L'Etranger*: Samples of a Twentieth-Century Atmosphere," *Symposium,* XII (Spring-Fall, 1958), 19–35.

9. ————. "To Him Sisyphus Symbolized Man," *Saturday Review,* XLV (March 10, 1962), 20.

10. VIGGIANI, CARL A. "Camus' *L'Etranger,*" *PMLA,* LXXI, V (December, 1956), 865–87.

Index